Instagram
POWER

Instagram

POWER

Build Your Brand and
Reach More Customers with
the Power of Pictures

JASON G. MILES

NEW YORK   CHICAGO   SAN FRANCISCO
ATHENS   LONDON   MADRID
MEXICO CITY   MILAN   NEW DELHI
SINGAPORE   SYDNEY   TORONTO

  6 7 8 9 0   QFR/QFR   1 9 8 7 6 5

ISBN 978-0-07-182700-3
MHID   0-07-182700-5

e-ISBN 978-0-07-182701-0
e-MHID   0-07-182701-3

Design by Lee Fukui and Mauna Eichner

McGraw-Hill Education books are available at special quantity discounts to use as premiums and sales promotions or for use in corporate training programs. To contact a representative, please visit the Contact Us pages at www.mhprofessional.com.

To Janice Hammond
and the other staff members of
the Lincoln Elementary Learning Center
and to my mother

In fourth grade, I moved to a new school, Lincoln Elementary in Yuba City, California. The teachers there quickly discovered that I hadn't been taught how to read or write adequately. It turned out that I was profoundly behind the other kids in my grade level, so each day for most of the class periods I would go to the Learning Center instead of the regular classrooms. It was a humiliating three years. My only comfort was recess, where I was officially known as the second fastest runner in the school. I hoped my speed on the field could make up for my slowness in the classroom. Of course, it didn't.

One teacher in the learning center, Janice Hammond, was particularly helpful. She showed me the ropes and made reading and writing fun. Then toward the end of the sixth grade, I passed the tests necessary to be put back into the general population. Shortly after, my mom read one of my school writing assignments and said, "Jason, you're a writer." I'll never forget that moment. Those words had power and sank in pretty deep. So thanks, Janice Hammond and the other Learning Center staff members at Lincoln Elementary; I owe you a special debt of gratitude. You showed me that writing is fun. It's a lesson that has served me really well. And thanks, Barbara Miles, for telling me I was a writer. You have been the most encouraging person in my life. I'll always be grateful for all you've done for me.

Contents

Part 2
MARKETING ON INSTAGRAM

Part 3
BONDING AND BRANDING ON INSTAGRAM

Chapter 8 Instant Buying Decisions on Instagram   83

Chapter 9 Instagram for Nonprofits and Service Providers   93

Chapter 10 Branding on Instagram   105

Part 4
SELLING ON INSTAGRAM

Chapter 11 Display Ads on Instagram   117

Part 5
INTEGRATING INSTAGRAM INTO YOUR ONLINE MARKETING

Part 6
TOOLS FOR LEVERAGING YOUR INSTAGRAM EXPERIENCE

Acknowledgments

This book would not have been possible without the wisdom and guidance of my agent, Marilyn Allen. Marilyn, thank you for providing practical advice and encouragement. It is an honor to be your client. Thank you, Janie Kliever, for helping me clean up this manuscript and get it ready to submit. You are an incredibly talented writer! I'm also grateful for my gracious prereaders, including Alejandro Reyes and Makena Miles. You saw the ugliest version of this book and provided very helpful feedback. Thank you also to my gracious coworkers at Northwest University for your patience and grace, as I took a lot of Fridays off in order to finish this book. Finally, I want to thank my beautiful and talented wife, Cinnamon Miles. You are the best thing that has ever happened to me, and I love you with all my heart.

Introduction

The world is migrating to smart mobile devices. Are you ready? These powerful new handheld tools include iPhones, iPads, Kindles, and similar Internet-enabled products. The worldwide adoption of these web-enabled tools is revolutionizing the online experience, including social media marketing.

Chances are, most people you know have a smartphone and several "i" products, too. How people access your website is shifting radically. In the fourth quarter of 2011, we saw a simple illustration of this fact that might surprise you. On September 9, 2012, CNNMoney.com reported that Apple's revenue from iPhone sales alone exceeded all of Microsoft's product lines combined. iPhone revenue for the 12 months prior was $74.3 billion, whereas Microsoft revenue was $73 billion. The iPhone business, if it were a stand-alone company, would be a Fortune 500 powerhouse. It would appear that the once dominant computer giant Microsoft and all that it represents is being dwarfed by smartphones, not to mention tablets such as the iPad and Kindle Fire.

How does Instagram fit into this picture? This book is about leveraging the first social media site "born mobile" to create your first mobile marketing campaign. Instagram is your gateway drug to becoming a hard-core mobile marketer.

In the fall of 2012, Instagram surpassed 100 million users and shocked marketers into realizing that this massive migration to mobile is real—and is happening more quickly than we might have expected. You might be wondering, *Why exactly should I learn how to use Instagram to market my business?* It's a good question and one that you shouldn't ignore. You need to decide if migrating to mobile is right for you. We are all in some form of social media overload, aren't we? So adding another social media site, even if it is low maintenance, can seem like a burden.

At my company, Liberty Jane Clothing, we decided it was important for us to be on Instagram after learning a set of surprising facts. This book chronicles our journey as well as the journey of other early adopters who are seeing solid success as a result of their Instagram work. Wondering what those facts were? Ready for a pop quiz? Let's see how well you do answering these questions:

1. How many cell phones exist worldwide?

2. How many of those are smartphones (i.e., capable of Internet browsing)?

3. How fast did the percentage of smartphones grow in 2012?

4. What percentage of U.S. adults owned a tablet or e-reader in 2009, and what did that number grow to in 2012?

5. By 2013, what is the expected number of tablet users?

6. Does Internet traffic from mobile devices exceed that of desktop web surfers in any large country?

7. What percentage of overall Internet traffic comes from smartphones?

8. Which is faster, the 4G LTE mobile network or high-speed DSL for your home?

9. On Black Friday 2012, what percentage of shopping occurred on mobile devices, and what was that number two years prior?

Let's see how you did answering the quiz and walk through the answers to these questions together. You might be surprised at the results.

■ **Question:** How many cell phones exist worldwide?

Answer: According to analyst Mary Meeker, at the end of 2012 there were 5 billion cell phones in use globally. She published the findings in her annual Global Trends Report. The planet has 7 billion people, but many of them are children. So while it is certainly true that not everyone on the planet has a cell phone, most certainly do. For marketers, this fact is not only shocking but also instructive.

I first realized how prevalent and powerful mobile phones were in 2008 when I went to the tiny mountain kingdom of Lesotho in southern Africa. I saw very poor women in extremely rural areas walking in a single-file line up to the top of a small hilltop. When I asked what they were doing, I was told they were walking up to the high ground to get a good cell signal to make a call. I was fascinated. There was no landline phone service in these areas and no electric utility providers. We were in the middle of nowhere, and yet cell phone technology had changed these ladies' lives.

I decided I had to learn more, so I met with several women who were HIV/AIDS caregivers in their community. I asked them through a translator if they used a cell phone, and they all said yes. I asked them if they had their phones on them, and again they all said yes. Then they reached into their blouses and pulled their cell phones out. Their practice was to carry their cell phones in their bras and pull them out as needed. They had a community system of using car batteries to charge their phones. It was a system that worked for them and enabled easy communication. That was more than five years ago now. I can only imagine how things have changed and how they will change in the next few years.

■ **Question:** How many of those are smartphones?

Answer: In her report, Mary Meeker went on to state that 1 billion of the phones on the planet are smartphones.

■ **Question:** How fast did the percentage of smartphones grow in 2012?

Answer: Mary Meeker noted that smartphone adoption grew in 2012 at a rate of 42 percent and that the trend is predicted to continue. Imagine how our HIV/AIDS community caregivers are going to respond when they have smartphones. Will they be able to afford the data plan? If they could, I can only imagine Siri on an iPhone trying to answer complicated questions related to their work.

- **Question:** What percentage of U.S. adults owned a tablet or e-reader in 2009, and what did that number grow to in 2012?

  Answer: It's not just smartphones that are changing the world. Tablets are a whole new option as well. In 2012, roughly 29 percent of U.S. adults own a tablet or e-reader, up from 2 percent less than three years previous (Meeker). By 2013, the number of U.S. tablet users is expected to reach 99 million, according to eMarketer.com. That is roughly 33 percent of the population. So what is the conclusion? Bob Parsons, CEO of GoDaddy.com, says "It's a fact that the personal computer as we know it today is going to go the way of the eight-track tape."

- **Question:** What percentage of overall Internet traffic comes from smartphones?

  Answer: In India, mobile Internet traffic surpassed desktop traffic in May 2012 (Meeker). That trend is occurring in other countries as well and will continue to become the new normal. It is not an exaggeration to say that the "current normal" web surfing experience will soon be a mobile experience.

- **Question:** Which is faster, the 4G LTE mobile network or high-speed DSL for your home?

  Answer: According to digitaltrends.com, in head-to-head comparisons of which Internet services were the fastest, the Verizon 4G LTE network performed better than high-speed DSL. It was not as good as the top-tier cable services, but price is a significant factor, so the conclusion was that "there is no question that cable is the faster, if you can afford the upper tiers . . . For the best deal, we ended up preferring Verizon LTE for a steady 12–15 Mbps connection speed and smooth video."

- **Question:** What percentage of overall Internet traffic comes from smartphones?

Answer: Although there are conflicting estimates, the amount of Internet traffic that is mobile based is remarkable and growing quickly. In May 2012, Chitika, an online advertising network, reported that roughly 20 percent of U.S. and Canadian Internet traffic now comes from mobile devices. Mary Meeker reported similar findings and said that in December 2009, Internet traffic coming from mobile devices was reportedly just 1 percent, but that three years later, that number had grown to 13 percent. So the experts are saying between 13 and 20 percent of all Internet traffic is mobile traffic.

I didn't believe those numbers were accurate. They seemed way too high. So I looked into our company's website statistics and found out some startling facts. Our primary e-commerce site has roughly 500,000 page views a month with close to 100,000 visitors. It's not big by corporate standards, but it's a large enough data set to get some good insight into what is happening. I'll save those findings for a more complete discussion on this topic in Chapter 18.

- **Question:** On Black Friday 2012, what percentage of shopping occurred on mobile devices, and what was that number two years prior?

Answer: If there is one national sales holiday in the United States that should give us good insight into this trend toward mobile devices, it's Black Friday. Traditionally, the day after Thanksgiving is a massive selling event. On Black Friday of 2010, 6 percent of online shopping occurred on a mobile device. On Black Friday of 2012, that number skyrocketed to 24 percent. Within a few years, mobile shopping could be the primary way in which consumers participate in Black Friday online sales.

The Shift in Social Behavior

This is all interesting, and possibly even shocking, but you might be asking, *How does this relate to a book about marketing on Instagram?* The answer is simple. As mentioned at the beginning of this Introduction, Instagram is the first social media site born mobile. While most social networks have a mobile app that allows users to access their accounts effectively, Instagram was conceived and created exclusively for that purpose. Learn Instagram marketing, and you'll be well on your way to learning the whole new world of mobile marketing.

In the upcoming chapters, you'll learn:

- How to get up and running on Instagram
- How to create a marketing plan
- How to leverage the social networking attributes of Instagram
- How to use the site effectively for advertising
- How to launch products
- How to measure and track all your work

Instagram provides an opportunity for you to bring your company into the new mobile revolution without complexity or drama. So keep reading and let's see how quickly we can get your Instagram marketing efforts up and running.

THE MOBILE MIGRATION

The Mobile Native

*I*nstagram is the breakout social network of the iPhone revolution. In less than two years, it has grown into a full-fledged social network that boasts more than 100 million users. In August 2012, Instagram passed Twitter in terms of daily active users on mobile devices (comScore). The pace of user adoption is staggering. In a single six-month period, Instagram went from 887,000 daily active users to 7.3 million (comScore).

Marketers have not been slow to leverage the new tool, as over 50 percent of top brands are now using Instagram (Marketing Land). Ben & Jerry's Homemade ice cream company is a good example of how smart marketers are leveraging this new platform. Ben & Jerry's is asking its fans to "capture euphoria" and share it on Instagram. How do you do that? You simply take a picture with your Ben & Jerry's ice cream, upload it to Instagram, and include the hashtag #captureeuphoria. Don't worry; we'll explain how hashtags work throughout the course of this book. When Ben & Jerry's customers upload a picture, it is automatically added to a special collection of thousands of fan photos. The Ben & Jerry's team will then use 20 of the photos as part of local print advertising campaigns, making those Instagram contributors local celebrities.

It seems clear that the marketing battlefield has shifted again. Mobile devices are the new place to be. In the 1990s, offline businesses like ice cream shops raced to develop websites to get a competitive edge over each other.

In the 2000s, those same companies raced to get a presence on the social networks; Facebook was their home base. They worked hard to find ways to engage their customers in conversations and contests. The goal was to build a social community around their brands.

In this new decade, those same companies are racing to migrate their efforts to mobile devices. As smartphones become more commonplace and alternative mobile devices like tablets grow in popularity, the rationale for mobile marketing becomes stronger. When the competition is doing mobile marketing, the pressure to operate in the new environment intensifies.

Additionally, as new apps like Instagram emerge, the marketing itself becomes very straightforward. Smart marketers have recognized that many of the same strategies that work effectively on other platforms work just as well or better on Instagram. It turns out that effective mobile marketing isn't that foreign after all.

Why are so many marketers excited about Instagram? It's the first significant social network built specifically to work on a mobile device. It's a pioneer in that regard. Whereas Facebook, Twitter, and Pinterest were born on the web and adapted to mobile devices, Instagram is a mobile native. Surprisingly, Twitter didn't have a smartphone app until four years after it was founded. While it was based on text messaging, it was envisioned as a microblogging tool, not a smartphone tool. Instagram's functionality was designed for ease of use on the iPhone and other Apple products, and it has subsequently been rolled out for Android devices. While Instagram recently added a website version of the app for user profiles, the functionality all resides on mobile devices. The website version allows for simple viewing of the content and not much more.

POWER TIP

A *mobile device* is a reference to any type of mobile phone or similar device, such as an iPod Touch, iPad, or other tablet that uses cellular technology.

Why does it help marketers that Instagram was born on a mobile device and is exclusively mobile in nature? It's a fairly simple answer:

it was designed to do one thing very elegantly—share photos. That simplicity of focus has real power.

The App Revolution

In 2007, the iPhone revolutionized the phone industry and created a new standard for phone technology. The smartphone got smarter. Buttons were out, and touch screens were in. This was more than a leap in technology; it created a new type of user engagement with phones. People expected their phones to serve as fully functional devices that seamlessly worked with the Internet, provided additional tools like a camera, and allowed them to constantly monitor e-mail and social media conversations. The bar had been permanently raised.

On July 11, 2008, as part of the iPhone 2.0 release, Apple launched the App Store, a store accessed on the iPhone that allows users to install third-party applications on their phones without ever connecting to a computer. Apps became a vital part of the iPhone revolution, and over 1 billion were downloaded in the first year.

This new ecosystem quickly fostered a booming industry. Third-party developers could create an app, upload it to the App Store, and, if they were lucky, see massive revenue start to roll in. Applications were developed for all sorts of user purposes, and although the games category led the way, other applications found their place too.

Apple was quick to christen the new catchphrase for this mobile revolution—"There's an app for that" became the mantra. This catchphrase became the natural response to almost any question that came to mind. The clever Apple marketers methodically drove home the statement in ad after ad, ensuring that people knew that if they had a problem, the App Store had a solution. Apple even went so far as to trademark the saying so that other competitors couldn't use it.

According to CNET, Apple had over 700,000 apps available for its operating system as of October 2012, and Google had that same number for its Android operating system, which has grown to become the primary rival to the Apple ecosystem. Even Microsoft has 120,000 apps available for its smartphone operating system. The three systems were all clearly working hard to rapidly expand the options available for their users.

Your Tribe Is Sharing Photos

In 2008, Seth Godin introduced us all to the concept of "tribes" and declared that marketers must lead a tribe with the permission and respect of the followers. So regardless of whether you've identified your tribe or not, your tribe is taking and sharing photos at a phenomenal rate. Your customers, fans, followers, and friends are jumping into Instagram. You might not know them, but if you share their interests, then you have an opportunity to engage with them. They are snapping photos of things they want, products they love, and places they visit. They are sharing their lives via Instagram. The only question is, *Are you going to join them on this new platform and begin to shape their experience?*

It shouldn't surprise us that taking and sharing photos is a national pastime; it has been incredibly popular since 1885 when George Eastman started manufacturing paper film. From the early days of black-and-white photography to today, the quest to capture life through pictures has been an unwavering human addiction. The beauty of this newest evolution of the hobby is that smart marketers can participate in creative and engaging ways to promote their brands.

The evolution of photography occurred in several specific stages. First there were images produced on paper, and with them the modern art of photography was born. Photo albums abounded. Next came the popularization of the slide show, the technological breakthrough that every brother-in-law hated. The invitation "Let me set up the slide projector to show you our vacation pictures" became a dreaded after-dinner comment. Then came the instant camera revolution. The Polaroid Corporation did a tremendous job profiting from that wave of photography enthusiasm. Finally, this was followed by digital photography and the use of images stored on computers. Film and film cameras became relics. In this latest evolution, the integration of digital photography and social sharing has become a reality.

How popular is sharing images on Instagram? Recent statistics indicate that roughly 5 million images are shared every day. In the first two years of Instagram's existence, over 4 billion images were shared. This rate of sharing will compound as the rate of new users continues to grow.

What Can You Do with Instagram?

If you're not familiar with the Instagram app yet, then let's go over the basic user functionality now; then in Chapter 2 we'll walk you through the process of getting up and running quickly. The goal of this book is to focus on the marketing opportunities available via Instagram, so we'll only spend one chapter on the basic functionality of the site. It's important to remember that as a marketer, you are using Instagram differently than a personal user would. There is a big difference between your goals on the site and the goals of your customers.

Instagram leverages your smartphone's camera and image library, allowing you to choose a picture or video and apply camera effects to it. The effects include things like making the picture black and white, cropping it, adding a border, or saturating the image so the colors pop. You can always simply share an image in an unedited format as well. According to the site, almost half of all images are shared with no editing effects applied.

POWER TIP

A *hashtag* is represented by the "#" preceding a word or preceding several words without spaces in between them. It allows simplecategorization to be applied to an image. Anyone can make a hashtag.

Once you've decided about how the image should be edited, you can add a description. The description can include plain text, or it can include a hashtag. Hashtags provide an easy way to categorize your images. Chris Messina, a Twitter user who wanted a way to help categorize conversations, originally created the hashtag in 2007. The hashtag system has been seamlessly integrated into Instagram for easy categorization.

Hashtags also allow you to expand the reach of your image far beyond your own list of followers, so that anyone interested in that topic can see your image by simply searching for that hashtag. For example, when we share an image that has the message "Red JANES coming soon to Liberty Jane Clothing #libertyjane #americangirldoll," it not only will go to our followers, but will also be visible to anyone searching for the hashtag #libertyjane or the hashtag #americangirldoll, as in Figure 1.1.

Figure 1.1 Images with captions that include a hashtag will go to a broader audience.

With a nice picture and a meaningful description, you're now ready to share the image. By finishing the upload process, your image is automatically shared with everyone who follows you on Instagram. Likewise, their images are made available to you when they upload a picture.

Once an image is shared, several social media standard behaviors can be used to engage with the image. We will discuss how to leverage these for social engagement in greater detail in later chapters, but for now we'll simply list them. They include:

- **Liking.** You can like the image as an expression of support.

- **Commenting.** You can leave a comment on a picture to join the conversation and make a statement. Your comments can include hashtags.

- **Sharing.** You can tweet about the images. Or if you uploaded the image yourself, you can share it to your Facebook account.

But Instagram has some limitations that might surprise you. At the time of this writing, there are a few things that you cannot do that you might expect to be able to do. They include:

- Adding a "clickable" URL in the description.

- Editing your description once it is uploaded.

- Adding a clickable URL in a comment.

- Sharing an image that you like with your followers. This functionality, popularized by Pinterest, is not a feature of Instagram.

Now that you know what Instagram is and the history of the social network, let's look at how my small business is using it to effectively engage with our tribe. Throughout this book, I'll use many business examples, and we'll focus together on various industries and niches so that you get a solid set of examples to learn from. But for this first chapter, I thought we should look at my own business as the example. Don't worry; we aren't trying to sell you anything. By sharing how we use Instagram, you get to know the following:

1. We are actually using Instagram effectively to grow our revenue for our small business.

2. This book is filled with best practices that are battle-tested and have been learned the hard way in the real world of competitive marketing. I'm not simply piling up social media platitudes and adapting them to Instagram. I am sharing from experience, not from theory.

3. I am an entrepreneur first and an author second. I don't consider myself a social media expert; I consider myself a marketer learning new things each day.

Up Close with Liberty Jane Clothing

Liberty Jane Clothing is my thriving six-figure small business. We started on eBay in 2008 and have grown by leveraging the power of social media. Instagram has become a primary part of our social media strategy.

We design and sell in the doll clothes category, offering both phys-ical and digital products. Our primary e-commerce site is Liberty Jane Patterns, with over 200,000 digital guidebooks downloaded to date and monthly page views exceeding 400,000.

Our social media work began on YouTube in 2008. We worked hard to create fun and interesting design contests and engage with our com-munity of prospects. It turned out that our tribe likes to hang out on YouTube, so we started there. Today we have over 8,500 subscribers on our YouTube channel and over 1.5 million video views. We've lever-aged that strength into the other social platforms (see Figure 1.2). Our next step was e-mail marketing, where we learned the power of driving direct traffic to our sites via newsletters. Our Facebook fan page came after that. We've worked hard and advertised extensively in order to get over 23,000 "likers" (formerly called fans) on Facebook. In 2011, we launched our Pinterest profile and quickly saw that site become our top source of social traffic. To document our Pinterest lessons, I cowrote the Amazon bestselling book *Pinterest Power*.

Figure 1.2 The Liberty Jane Clothing social reach

In 2012, we launched our Instagram profile and began learning how to engage with our tribe on the site. Our initial marketing strategy in-cluded six steps:

1. We began our Instagram work by sharing pictures of products from a "behind-the-scenes" perspective. Our goal was to al-low our followers to see an insider's view of our work. The idea of

being a "visual insider" seemed like an appealing concept to our prospects and customers.

2. We began exploring the concept of using Instagram as a tool to enable a visual product launch. I'll outline this strategy further in Chapter 5. The visual product launch concept has become a significant strategy for us.

3. We took our YouTube contest strategy and adapted it to Instagram. Our Instagram design contest was an effective engagement tool and helped expand our reach significantly. I'll outline this approach in Chapter 12.

4. We integrated Instagram into our other websites, including our Facebook fan page and our company website. I will walk through the details of how to do this effectively in Chapters 14 and 15.

5. We started systematically asking our existing customers, fans, and followers to follow us on Instagram. Our reasoning was that if they joined us on Instagram, they could introduce their friends to us.

6. We started exploring the hashtags associated with our niche and participating in the ongoing conversations. We started finding and following like-minded people.

The Instagram Advantage

Three advantages immediately stand out when it comes to Instagram versus other social media sites:

- Instagram works flawlessly on mobile phones. While other sites such as Facebook, Twitter, and Pinterest all have an app, Instagram is the only one that was born on the mobile phone and works flawlessly in that environment.

- Instagram, like Pinterest, is "social media lite." It is not based on conversations, so the upkeep is much more achievable compared with a conversation-intensive platform like Facebook or Twitter.

- Similarly to YouTube and Pinterest, there is a longer shelf life for content than there is on Facebook and Twitter. When you upload an image on Instagram, it will be readily available for your followers to view for a very long time.

If you're ready to become an Instagram marketer, then read on. In the upcoming chapters we'll dive deeply into effective marketing campaigns, we'll hear from the creative marketers that put the campaigns together, and we'll break down their strategies into simple action steps so you know exactly what to do to get started.

THE SNAPSHOT

(1) Instagram is the first social network that grew to massive scale without a desktop version. It's a mobile native. (2) Instagram can easily be your entry into mobile marketing. (3) Instagram is a social media platform that doesn't require very much conversation. (4) Instagram uses the hashtag system of categorization, similarly to what Twitter, Google+, and Pinterest use.

Chapter
2

Get Clicking on Instagram

etting started with Instagram is simple. The main thing to remember is that you manage your Instagram efforts from your
phone, not from your computer. The process is slightly different
for an iPhone user versus an Android phone user. We will point out the
differences between the two versions throughout this chapter.

As with all new software tools, there is a learning curve that you
struggle through until you feel confident with the tool. Don't worry;
you'll get to that point fairly quickly with Instagram. It is a simple
system to use. There is also an excellent Help Center at http://help
.instagram.com.

Signing Up for an Instagram Account

The Instagram iPhone app is available for iPhone users from the App
Store (see Figure 2.1). For Android phone users, it is available from
Google Play.

Figure 2.1 Search for Instagram in the App Store; or for Android Phones, search in Google Play.

Here are the steps involved in getting the app and registering for a new account on an iPhone:

1. In the App Store search bar, type in "Instagram."

2. Click Install.

3. After the app is installed, click Open.

4. Choose the Register button to create your new account.

5. Choose a user name and password. Your user name must be available, which can sometimes be tricky. Ideally, your preferred user name will be available. If you are establishing an account for your business, this is where you would enter your company's name.

6. Create a profile. This can be expedited if you let Instagram access your Facebook information. That choice is presented in the Profile section.

7. After you read the Instagram Terms of Service (TOS) and Privacy Policy, click Done. By clicking Done, you are agreeing to these important documents.

A Marketer's View of the Terms of Service

We won't bore you with an in-depth look at these documents, but the TOS and Privacy Policy are the documents that govern Instagram's basic behavior and your understanding of your rights related to the site. These documents outline what you can and cannot do on the site. As a marketer, you want to pay particular attention to the aspects of the documents that relate to your use for marketing purposes. It is foolish to operate on a site without understanding what you can and cannot do. Simply seeing another marketer do something is no guarantee that it is an appropriate action.

Because the TOS and Privacy Policy are updated over time, you'll want to search the documents regularly to see if they add language that might impact you. You don't want to conduct marketing activities on a social site if the TOS forbid it. One easy way to audit the document is to go to the TOS web page, then use your computer's find function (Command+F on a Mac or Ctrl+F on a PC), and search for specific terms, such as *business*, *contest*, or *promotions.*

In December 2012, there was a major uproar related to a proposed Instagram TOS change and the language it included. Fortunately, the Instagram team immediately responded to user sentiment and backtracked. But future revisions are inevitable. Here is our list of topics we pay particular attention to, as they relate to marketing on any social network, including Instagram:

1. Terms related to the ownership of the content uploaded to the site. This was the issue that created such uproar in December 2012. You'll want to monitor this issue to ensure that the terms related to content ownership are not unappealing for business use. According to the TOS as of January 13, 2013, Instagram claims no ownership of images uploaded.

2. Terms related to conducting promotions, giveaways, or contests on the site. Facebook's contest-related terms are very well documented, and some would say strict; whereas on Instagram, as of January 13, 2013, the TOS makes no mention of contests. Marketers generally view this as permission to conduct contests. But Instagram's view on contests could change, as its parent company, Facebook, may very well influence this policy.

3. Terms related to business use, such as advertising.

4. Terms related to what the company will do when your account is suspended or terminated. This is helpful to know because it can easily happen. For example, on August 4, 2011, we had our Facebook fan page suspended and had to work through a process of having it reinstated. Believe me, after four years of marketing on Facebook, paying thousands of dollars to advertise our fan page, and seeing it grow to over 10,000 fans, it can be stressful to see it disappear. We hadn't done anything wrong, and within a few days we were back in action.

5. The steps to take to close your account if you decide to no longer use the service.

6. The process for reporting abuse, copyright infringement, or your account being hacked.

Basic App Navigation

There are five primary screens in Instagram that you will learn to navigate. The navigation is very simple and easy to understand. Part of the beauty of Instagram being designed to work on a phone is that the choices are simple, the navigation path is clear, and opportunities to get lost are minimized.

The primary navigation menu rests at the bottom of the screen almost constantly, so it is difficult to feel lost. Using the primary navigation menu as your constant frame of reference allows you to quickly navigate among the five screens. The only time the navigation menu is not at the bottom of the screen is when the Camera tab is in use.

Let's explore each of the five tabs to discover how they work and what they are designed to do. Remember, there are more extensive online tutorials and tips at http://help.instagram.com.

The Home Tab

The Home tab allows you to see a feed of the latest pictures added by either you or the people you follow (see Figure 2.2). On the Home tab you can like and comment on these pictures quickly and easily. In addition to showing the picture, the Home tab also shows the number of likes an image has received and the description entered by the author. As space allows, it will also show comments.

Figure 2.2 The Instagram Home tab provides a feed of recent images uploaded by you or the people you follow.

The Explore Tab

The Explore tab allows you to discover new Instagram users that you might like to follow and topics that are related to your industry or interests. In older versions of Instagram, this was referred to as the Popular tab. It still functions in that manner. Let's talk about being popular on the Explore tab; then we'll discuss other ways you can use this tab effectively.

POWER TIP

Use the Explore tab functionality to find people in your niche or industry so you can start following them quickly. Look to see whom they are following and who is following them.

Popular Images on the Explore Tab

Having an image displayed at the top of the Explore tab can boost your Instagram profile dramatically, allowing more people to learn about you quickly. Your followers also receive a message that says, "[Your Company's] photo made it to the popular page," which helps the image gain even more exposure. Although Instagram doesn't reveal the exact methodology for getting an image into this enviable position, most people believe it is a combination of several factors. Blogger Chris Smith suggests that the factors include:

1. The number of likes you get from your followers within the first 10 to 20 minutes of posting the image.

2. The relative competition at the time. Each image is competing against other images in real time. As with any type of popularity system, sometimes the competition is overly strong, and sometimes it happens to be weak.

3. The number of likes you receive from your followers compared with those from nonfollowers. Although people who find it by looking at a hashtag can like your image, it appears that more relative weight is given to likes that come from your followers.

Other Ways to Use the Explore Tab

Users can navigate using the Explore tab in several ways (see Figure 2.3). Let's review them briefly. First, you can simply browse the grid of pictures that Instagram provides to you. These users may or may not be of interest to you. They are presented because they are popular, but that doesn't necessarily make them a good candidate for you to follow.

Figure 2.3 The Explore tab allows you to search for users and hashtags.

Second, you can search for specific users in the search bar, like "Liberty Jane Clothing." Searching for companies that are key players in your niche or industry is probably a wise idea. Or you can search for the celebrities that dominate your niche.

Third, you can search for specific hashtags, like "#libertyjane." Don't worry; we'll discuss hashtags in much greater detail in Chapter 3. If you search for a hashtag, you'll see the images that have been tagged and the Instagram users who shared them. Following the Instagram users who regularly use hashtags related to your industry is probably a wise first step.

The Camera Tab

The Camera tab provides an alternative method of accessing your phone's camera. Ultimately, it is your choice about whether this method of accessing your phone's camera is useful to you or whether you use your phone's primary camera tool. The rationale for including this function in the Instagram app is that it allows you to go from picture taking to picture editing without ever leaving the app (see Figure 2.4).

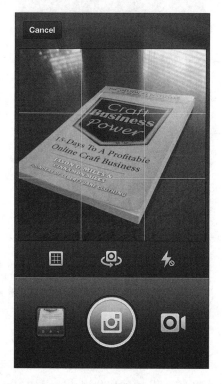

Figure 2.4 The Instagram Camera tab allows you to take pictures and video directly from Instagram.

Along the top of the Camera tab there are three options. You can turn on a simple grid that is designed to help you line up your image. You can turn the camera's flash on or off or allow it to be in auto-detect mode. Finally, you can switch between your phone's front camera and rear camera.

In addition to using the camera to take a picture, you can also access your camera's image library from the Camera tab. Once you either take a picture or choose an image from your image library, you will move to an editing screen.

The Instagram editing screen allows you to conduct two primary activities. First, you can make edits to the image and put it into the final visual form you want to use. Second, you can prepare the information that will accompany your image. Both these activities are vitally important for marketing purposes. Social impact is a combination of imagery and messaging. Your ultimate success on Instagram will depend largely on the choices you make in these two categories. Let's take a closer look at each topic. Some of these topics will be the subject of later chapters in this book, so in those cases we'll briefly touch on the topic here.

Modifying Your Image

Instagram is about images, so it stands to reason that regardless of whatever else you want to accomplish by way of marketing goals, you also need to produce images that are very appealing to your followers. That will be different in different niches and categories, but the basics of professional photography must be mentioned. Let's walk through the options available for editing your images in the Camera tab section of Instagram:

1. **Crop your image.** There are three primary objectives when cropping an image. First, you want to narrow the focus and decide what element of the image should be the primary focal point. Second, you want to intentionally remove any unwanted elements from the image. Finally, you want to correct composition problems and align your image using the rule of thirds, which states that images are more interesting if placed off-center. The Instagram cropping feature automatically provides the grid that indicates the one-third lines.

2. **Rotate the image.** Some images can be rotated to improve the presentation. This won't work for too many types of images, but it comes in handy if you held your phone sideways when you took your picture and the image is saved at a 90° angle. This function allows you to rotate it back into the standard view.

3. **Add a border.** In some cases, particularly when an image has a lot of white space on the sides, it is more attractive with a border applied.

4. **Add a blur effect.** Good portraiture frequently uses a depth-of-field technique in which part of the image is in focus and part of the image is blurry. You can achieve a similar effect by using Instagram's blur-effect options.

5. **Add a Lux effect.** High-dynamic-range (HDR) photos are very popular. The Instagram Lux effect allows you to achieve a similar result, which makes your images much more vibrant.

6. **Add a filter.** There are numerous filters to choose from to achieve various results. Many times, filters can improve a mediocre picture substantially. Filters can help correct problems with your image's lighting or white balance. Don't feel compelled to use a filter if one is not needed. Many Instagram users appreciate seeing unedited photos, and if your image is good, then simply skip adding any filter.

Preparing the Metadata

You can add metadata to your images that help your followers learn more about the image. Metadata is information that accompanies your image but is not actually visible on the image. Preparing the metadata includes:

1. **Adding a caption.** Your description of the image is a vital part of communicating more details about the image. We will cover this in greater detail in Chapter 11.

2. **Adding location details.** By having your Photo Map enabled, you can easily allow followers to see where your pictures were taken. Additionally, you can name locations to add even more detail.

3. **Adding hashtags.** A hashtag is a categorization system originally pioneered on Twitter. It is simply a word proceeded by the # sign—for example, #sunset. This allows the image to be included in the category of images that have the #sunset hashtag. There are lots of terrific marketing activities that can be done with hashtags. We'll discuss that in more detail in Chapter 3.

The News Feed Tab

The News Feed tab has two primary views (see Figure 2.5). The News view allows you to see the likes and comments that you've received most recently. It's a simple way to keep up-to-date on what your followers are doing related to you images and account. The Following view summarizes the recent activity of the people you are following. This allows you to keep up on what other people are liking and commenting on.

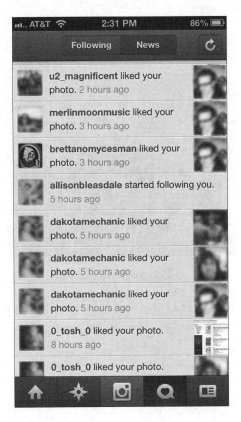

Figure 2.5 The News tab gives you updates on recent activity.

The Profile Tab

The Profile tab is the final tab located on the far right side of the navigation menu. It is probably the most important tab for marketers. All the functions related to account management are accessed through this tab (see Figure 2.6).

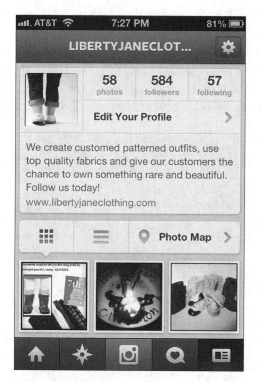

Figure 2.6 The Profile tab allows you to manage your account details.

The top right corner of the Profile tab has a gear button that accesses the Account Options section. In Account Options, you can do the following:

1. Find and invite friends.

2. View the photos you've liked.

3. Log out.

4. Modify your sharing settings, including how your account is connected to Facebook and other social media sites.

5. Manage your push notifications. Push notifications are e-mails you receive from Instagram when certain actions occur, such as when your images are liked or commented on.

6. Clear your search history.

7. Modify your privacy settings, including the option to require your approval before someone can follow you.

8. Manage how your photos are saved.

The top section of the Profile tab allows you to add a profile picture and see how many photos you've uploaded, how many followers you have, and how many people you are following. To add or edit a profile picture, you simply click on the image box and you're presented with a menu of options.

The center section of the Profile tab allows you to edit your profile details. In addition to adding an informative profile description, you can also add a link to your website, add a user name, change your password, and modify your privacy settings.

The Website Version of Your Instagram Profile

In late 2012, Instagram released a website version of its application. The domain name structure simply places the Instagram user name at the end of http://www.instagram.com—for example, http://www .instagram.com/libertyjaneclothing, as shown in Figure 2.7. In many ways, this opened the floodgates of creativity for marketers and brand managers. Let's look at the elements of the website version of your Instagram account.

Figure 2.7 The website version of your Instagram account is a useful tool.

The website version of your Instagram profile doesn't allow you to update your images, but you can make changes to your account, as well as follow people or like and comment on photos. The website version also gives you a website integration tool that you might find helpful—badges. You access the badges' functionality from the top-right-corner navigation menu. You can choose from a collection of nice Instagram icons that you use to link to your Instagram web profile. The badges section gives you the HTML code that you can cut and paste onto your website. There are certainly lots of ways to integrate Instagram into your website, and this is one very straightforward option.

Added Functionality

In Part 6, we'll discuss a whole collection of apps that can add functionality to your Instagram experience. But don't feel like you need to go beyond the basics to get up and running quickly. Now that we've reviewed the basics, in Chapter 3 we will explore how to leverage the power of hashtags to grow your Instagram impact.

THE SNAPSHOT

(1) Take the time to quickly learn about the five Instagram tabs and how they work. (2) Look at your website version, http://www.instagram.com/youruserprofilename, to see how your images look on a desktop computer. (3) Use the Explore tab to find people in your niche or industry to follow. (4) Start to consider how your profile image and description can effectively represent your work on Instagram.

Hashtags: Organizing a Chaotic World

Hashtags provide a way to organize and sort information inside a social media website. The concept was originally created in Twitter, and many social media websites have adopted the same methodology including Google+, Pinterest, and Instagram.

When you share a picture on Instagram and include a hashtag in the caption, then anyone looking at that hashtag via the Explore tab will see your image. The image feed in the Explore tab cascades with the newest content at the top, so if you include a very popular hashtag with your image, it will likely be at the top of that hashtag's feed for just a few seconds, but many people might still see it. If you include a less popular hashtag, it will stay on the first page of the feed for a longer period of time, but fewer people may ultimately see it.

Hashtags have enormous utility for creative marketers. Let's review a few of the powerful ways you can leverage the hashtag system:

1. You can create hashtags and use them creatively in your business.

2. You can use hashtags to research popular trends in your niche.

3. You can use hashtags to participate in conversations within your industry or niche.

4. You can identify new prospects using hashtags.

5. You can share your images with a much broader group of people than just your followers.

A Brief History of Hashtags

Twitter user Chris Messina created the concept of using the hashtag for social media conversations. On August 23, 2007, he tweeted a suggestion to use the # sign as a method of categorizing conversations within the site. His innovation didn't gain widespread acceptance immediately. People complained that the use of the # sign made the message difficult to read.

The system gained real social acceptance during the October 2007 San Diego wildfires. The hashtag #sandiegofire became the organizing phrase that enabled people to communicate quickly and conveniently. The method of using the # sign in front of a word or phrase, although distracting to people reading the message, proved very useful.

Twitter coined the name *hashtag*, and on July 1, 2009, the company began hyperlinking the hashtagged words together in search results, making the function of using hashtags very convenient. The list of social networks and related sites that have adopted this practice is fairly extensive. The best-known sites include Google+, Tumblr, Pinterest, and Instagram.

Creating Hashtags

Creating your own hashtags enables a nice collection of marketing activities, including leading conversations and creating topics that rally customers and interested prospects in ad hoc conversations and sharing. Being the thought leader also positions you as the leader of your tribe. Creating a hashtag for a specific customer purpose also gives you the opportunity to ask people to use that custom hashtag as a social media reply device. This approach is what powers most Instagram contests, which we'll cover more deeply in Chapter 12.

Hashtags can be set up by anyone simply using the # symbol before a word or phrase. You can use any hashtag you'd like without needing anyone's permission. As I was writing this chapter one evening, my wife started laughing out loud from the other room. I asked her what was so funny, and she said that Libby (our daughter) had just uploaded a picture of herself and made her own hashtag: #ishouldprobablybedoing somethingproductiverightnow. We laughed at the ingenuity and the sense of self-reflection and wondered if it might catch on. Feel free to check on Instagram. Hashtags should generally be one word, or maybe a brief phrase. Libby's is a monster to type into Instagram, but once you type it in one time, your phone will remember it and auto-populate it when you start typing it. Of course, it could be used in association with negative or inappropriate images, so time will tell whether it serves a useful social purpose on Instagram.

As a marketer, there are some best practices that you need to keep in mind when you start to consider how best to create and utilize hashtags. Let's review them briefly:

1. Be brief—use either one word or a short phrase.

2. Try to create a hashtag that is memorable and easily understood.

3. Check to make sure the hashtag is not open to multiple interpretations, or else it runs the risk of being used for the wrong purpose.

4. Check to make sure the hashtag is not already in use before creating it.

5. Don't create hashtags that include another company's brand or product name.

6. Remember that once you set up a hashtag, it becomes a communication tool for anyone to use. What you popularize, others can hijack. You cannot control its use.

Research Trends in Your Niche

Even in a tiny niche, like the doll clothes market, there are new topics, trends, and concepts being created all the time. New competitors come into the market, new events happen, and industry news comes and goes. By following thought leaders in your industry and watching their use of hashtags, you can quickly keep your finger on the pulse of trending topics. Because of the visual nature of Instagram, this type of research is even more helpful for product sellers because you can get a quick look at new items you might not otherwise see.

There are many sites online that document the top trending Instagram hashtags, and it is important to review them. According to http://www.tophashtags.com, the top 10 hashtags are:

1. #love

2. #instagood

3. #me

4. #cute

5. #tbt

6. #photooftheday

7. #instamood

8. #tweegram

9. #iphonesia

10. #picoftheday

But even more important than knowing the common hashtags is knowing the popular hashtags in your industry or niche. Those won't show up on general lists. They might be unique to your industry, and the best way to discover them is to search for the terms through Instagram's Explore tab until you discover what your niche's customers are commonly using. You can also use websites like http://top-hashtags.com/instagram/.

> **POWER TIP**
>
> Instead of simply using popular hashtags, research the hashtags that are commonly used in your niche or industry and use those. It's better to attract prospective customers that are interested in your industry than random people.

What do you do when you don't know the meaning of a hashtag? Visit http://www.tagdef.com or a similar site to learn the definitions of various tags. For example, you may have noticed on the top 10 list that hashtag 5 is #tbt. That stands for Throwback Thursday, which is a tradition on Instagram of sharing a picture on Thursday that is from years gone by.

Find Prospects Using Hashtags

You have an opportunity to identify people who are interested in your niche or industry. Simply look to see who is sharing pictures using the related hashtags. This is a significant opportunity that is easy to do.

Join in the Sharing

In some industries or niches, using the common hashtags can feel like a giant waste of time, and it might be. But in other niches, participating in the trending topics is a simple way to engage with prospective customers. You'll have to decide whether this is a good approach for your situation.

One indicator of whether your time will be well spent joining a conversation via a hashtag or using it for an Instagram image is whether you are (or your brand is) fairly well known and respected. If so, then you have an easy way to make a strong social impact. If not, then you'll need to work much harder to make yourself known, and you'll have to determine if that is time well spent. If you are a product marketer, the answer is probably a strong yes. If you are a service provider, then it might be yes or it might be no. As with all other forms of advertising, you probably need to take a long-term view and plan on sharing very faithfully before you start to see customers recognizing you and your work.

Cautionary Tales

As mentioned previously, companies have learned that hashtags can be hijacked and used for customer complaints. Hashtags are wild and free. Once created, they take on a power of their own. Creating a hashtag associated with your brand is the equivalent of setting up open-mic night on the Internet. Setting up a popular hashtag and giving it prominence through your other media channels, only to have it constantly used to trash your company, is a PR nightmare. Be careful to consider your brand's reputation in the marketplace and whether it might be wiser to simply participate in industry conversations rather than creating unique hashtags that can be used against you.

McDonald's and the #McDStories Hashtag

McDonald's learned this the hard way when it set up a Twitter hashtag campaign in January 2012. The initial hashtag it created was #MeetThe Farmers, which the company used effectively to share stories of healthy produce and locally sourced ingredients. McDonald's paid to promote the hashtag, so it gained wide prominence. But the second hashtag, #McDStories, was much more problematic.

Soon the hashtag was being used to share food poisoning stories, broadcast customer service complaints, mock the company with funny insults, and generally bash the brand. The anti-McDonald's sentiment turned into a competitive sport, and the hashtag was the ball. Twitter users took turns coming up with the most sarcastic 140 character messages they could, and happily tacked on the #McDStories hashtag to broadcast their messages.

The initial error was only one layer of the ordeal. Social media bloggers also took the opportunity to publicly correct the company on its approach. Not only did McDonald's receive mockery from the public; it received public criticism from social media marketers, too.

There are plenty of lessons to learn from the McDonald's story. Let's review them briefly:

1. A hashtag is a communication tool, and like any good tool, it can be used to build up or tear down. Hashtags are like a megaphone, and if you create one, it has power. If you take it a step further and advertise it on your other media channels, you give it even more prominence and power.

2. Crafting hashtags in a focused way that shapes the conversation in a direction of your choosing is wiser than making them more

general. The #MeetTheFarmers hashtag didn't provide an easy on-ramp to complaints like the #McDStories one did.

3. Your brand resides in the mind of the consumer. If you ask people to share their thoughts publicly, you might be surprised at the level of negativity. Don't expect them to be "on message." In social media, this inability to control the message is particularly problematic for larger brands that have negative consumer sentiment to deal with. It doesn't mean they shouldn't use social media; it means they should be careful how they structure the engagement.

Kenneth Cole and the #Cairo Hashtag

Brand managers don't have to create their own hashtags in order to run into problems. Fashion brand Kenneth Cole learned this lesson in the spring of 2011.

As part of its social media promotion efforts for its spring collection, the company tweeted out, "Millions are in uproar in #Cairo. Rumor is they heard our new spring collection is now available at http://bit.ly/KCairo-KC." The negative sentiment was immediate. This form of message is referred to as "hijacking a hashtag," and when an individual Twitter or Instagram user does it, it is not looked on favorably. When a brand does it, the backlash can be intense.

The negative sentiment in this case was heightened because of the seriousness of the #Cairo hashtag. It was being used in Egypt to coordinate communication for the express purpose of the overthrow of the government. Riots and intense conflict were raging. The power of the #Cairo hashtag for productive social change was in full effect. In other words, the world was watching.

The brand did apologize and worked to correct its course, but the misstep was a big enough mistake to become a cautionary tale that has been repeated relentlessly.

The Kenneth Cole story can teach us several great lessons:

1. Hashtags, once created, have intended uses that, although not documented anywhere, are socially understood by the majority of users. Using a hashtag in a way that deviates from how most people use it can provoke anger.

2. Marketers run the same risk in social media as they do in traditional marketing channels. If they share their marketing message in an inappropriate context, they'll create negative sentiment. The difference in the social media context is that the public has an equal voice and can respond immediately with a swift rebuke.

3. Hijacking a hashtag is about control of the concept. A crowd can take control pretty easily by the sheer volume of responses. But if you are a brand and you want to take control of a concept or use it for your own purposes, you really need to evaluate the context, the risk of failure, and the opportunity to be perceived negatively. There are very few cases in which this explosive approach can be used effectively.

Ben & Jerry's #captureeuphoria

Ben & Jerry's rolled out an incredibly creative and simple Instagram contest in November 2012. The elegance of the approach is something everyone can learn from. The company proved that an integrated marketing campaign that includes Instagram could engage customers and prospects in an innovative way.

The company asked customers to upload a picture and use the #captureeuphoria hashtag as they answered the question, "What does euphoria mean to you in relation to Ben & Jerry's Ice Cream?" The winning entrants would be featured in Ben & Jerry's advertising within their region of the country.

While the campaign garnered a lot of positive attention and seemed to be successful, it also served as a reminder to marketers everywhere that hashtags are uncontrollable. As you might guess, not all the 13,000+ participants remembered the "in relation to Ben & Jerry's Ice Cream" part of the contest description. So while there were many photos of ice cream cartons and happy customers, there were also plenty of images that were completely unrelated. Many of the hashtag's users seemed to be using it to expand the reach of their personal photos, not to participate in the contest.

Hashtag Dos and Don'ts

We hope these cautionary tales have helped clarify the importance of getting your plan nailed down when it comes to using hashtags. Let's review a list of best practices.

Hashtag Dos

1. Do take the time to research the hashtags associated with your industry and learn how they are best used.

2. Do participate in the use of hashtags to extend your message to a broad audience.

3. Do look to see who is using your niche or industry hashtags and follow them.

4. Do use caution when creating new hashtags to ensure you can shape the dialogue as much as possible.

5. Do create hashtags that are brief and easily understood.

6. Do use websites that help you learn about new hashtags and keep up on trending topics.

Hashtag Don'ts

1. Don't forget that hashtags are a tool that can be used to do damage.

2. Don't underestimate the negative sentiment that might be bottled up about your brand and unleashed via hashtags.

3. Don't create hashtags that are too general and open to broad interpretation or multiple meanings.

4. Don't use general trending hashtags for marketing purposes.

5. Don't create hashtags with brand names that you do not have express permission to manage.

6. Don't overuse hashtags. Most people suggest using between 2 and 10, but no more. Technically you can add up to 30, but that is not recommended unless you've really considered the impact. Adding a long list of hashtags could make you look a little too desperate.

THE SNAPSHOT

(1) Hashtags are a great tool for engaging with customers. (2) Include a few of the most relevant hashtags with your images. (3) Use hashtags to research your industry and connect with new prospects. (4) Remember that if you create a hashtag in association with your brand, anyone can use it, including haters.

Part 2

MARKETING ON INSTAGRAM

An Instagram Marketing Plan

People frequently say that social media is not the place to make sales. They say that social media sites are more about PR and goodwill than closing and selling. People say that your followers on social media will not accept your marketing tactics. I think the people making these comments fall into four categories:

1. Social media consultants who want to be paid to consult on the topic of social media marketing, but who don't want the pressure of being held accountable for revenue-related outcomes.

2. Business writers who have never run a business and have a general impression about how things really work, but no specific profit and loss experience.

3. People who are in a business category that does not lend itself to social media. They assume that all businesses are like theirs.

4. People who are in a business that could generate sales via social media, but who haven't learned how to do it, and so assume it cannot be done.

The truth is that most types of businesses can benefit from a social media plan and use social media as a key part of their sales cycle. If you're a businessperson and social media doesn't provide a way of making sales, then you shouldn't be doing it. It is too labor intensive, too time consuming, and too challenging to not have direct benefits. But for many businesses, social media is the perfect place to sell—if you know how to do it.

Should I Use Instagram?
The 5-10-20 Test

How can you determine if using Instagram is a productive use of your time? We can even extend this question to include other forms of social media such as Facebook, YouTube, Pinterest, and Twitter. Is using social media a productive use of your time? It really does depend on the niche you're in and your position in the market. I would propose the "5-10-20 test." It is a concept I developed to help people evaluate whether social media is right for them.

Does your business engage with more than five customers? Can you service more than that and grow as they are added? Some businesses only have one customer, such as the federal government, and therefore a social media presence is unnecessary. But even a business such as a custom homebuilder that works with one customer at a time will likely need a pipeline of prospective customers. The number of customers you will work with over the short term is one factor to consider.

Do you plan to launch more than 10 products in the short term? Even if you only have one customer, if you are launching products this frequently, then chances are you would benefit from a social presence and from fans or followers who appreciate what you do. If you're in an industry that is this product-centric, then chances are you have the opportunity to have a fan base that either loves your specific work or loves the industry or niche. Connecting with those people will likely add real business value.

Is a premium price point possible? If your brand is well known in your niche, would having a solid set of raving fans help add a pricing premium of 20 percent or more? That might be hard for you to predict, but you probably know if you're in a price-sensitive market niche. You probably also know where your pricing falls on the spectrum of possible prices. If you can position your product as an ultrapremium option in your market, then having a social media presence is a wise choice. Social proof is a significant factor in determining price, and social media is a simple way to acquire social proof.

> **POWER TIP**
>
> Use the 5-10-20 test to determine if a social media plan is worth your time. If so, then consider how Instagram can play a vital role.

How Does Instagram Compare with the Top Social Sites?

Instagram is a unique platform unlike any other social media site, but there are similarities, particularly to Twitter and Pinterest, that help us understand how selling can work. The biggest question in your mind should be, *Why would I use Instagram as part of my social media marketing strategy?*

The simplest answer to this question might be so that you have an effective mobile marketing strategy. In the past when someone said, "You should have a mobile phone strategy," people thought that meant having a texting or SMS (short message service) strategy, which required you to collect people's phone numbers. People are not too excited to give away their phone numbers—have you noticed? But if you're going to do marketing with the singular goal of engaging with people when they are on their smartphones, then an Instagram marketing campaign might be the easiest approach. So when your CEO says, "What's our mobile marketing approach?" you say, "We're really excited about mobile marketing—Instagram has been a fantastic tool for us. We are aggressively growing in that space, and our brand is very well positioned."

Before we discuss the marketing campaign, let's discuss how Instagram compares with other social media sites. For the sake of brevity, I am only going to compare Instagram with the top social networks. To make the comparisons consistent, I'll use four factors:

- **Time and energy required.** How much time does it take to maintain a solid presence on the site?

- **Follower expectations.** What do people expect you to do on the site in terms of good social etiquette?

- **Half-life of the content.** How long do followers engage with your content?

- **Virality.** How easy is it for your fans or followers to share your content across social media platforms?

Instagram Compared with Facebook

Because Instagram was acquired by Facebook in 2012, it is a good bet that Facebook will continue to offer integration and support options to boost the Instagram platform, so that's great. But when it comes to comparing them for marketing purposes, a few key differences emerge when we look at our factors:

- **Time and energy required.** Instagram is much less labor intensive than Facebook. Facebook is conversation intensive, while Instagram infrequently includes conversations. Facebook is a general social media tool, while Instagram is much more targeted, which in my view allows for much more targeted marketing efforts. That being said, if there is one social media platform everyone should be on, it is Facebook.

- **Follower expectations.** Followers on Instagram expect you to publish a few pictures a day—that's it. They appreciate it when you like their photo, and they are blown away when you leave a comment. Facebook followers, on the other hand, expect you to show up, say something, and be generally conversational with them. They expect real-time participation.

- **Half-life of the content.** Instagram images have a longer life expectancy than a status update on Facebook. They also have a better chance of attracting follower engagement than photos added on Facebook.

■ **Virality.** Both Instagram and Facebook are based on the idea of publishing to prompt action. You publish something, and people like it, comment on it, or share it. This happens equally on both sites.

Instagram Compared with YouTube

Instagram is more similar to YouTube than it is to Facebook. Your artistic endeavor has long-term value whether it is a video on YouTube or an image on Instagram. There is a real-time sharing element to Instagram that is not as prominent on YouTube, but overall, they are very similar. The key concept to remember is that picture taking is much more popular than video making. Reflect for a moment on your phone or PC hard drive. How many pictures do you have saved versus videos saved? The volume of images we take is enormous. As a marketer, that suggests to me that people may ultimately be engaged with Instagram much more frequently and for longer periods of time than with YouTube. I'm sure as the site develops, researchers will validate whether this theory is correct or not. When it comes to comparing them for marketing purposes, a few key differences emerge when we look at our factors:

■ **Time and energy required.** In terms of influencing your followers, Instagram's image-based sharing is not nearly as powerful as video messages. Then again, it is much simpler to take a nice product shot than it is to shoot and edit a video. Many marketers simply will not be comfortable with creating videos, but if you ask them to take a picture, they'll be happy to comply.

■ **Follower expectations.** On both Instagram and YouTube, followers have lower expectations of participation than on other social media sites. There is no expectation of timely or ongoing conversations.

■ **Half-life of the content.** Instagram and YouTube both have a very nice aspect of social sharing related to the half-life of the content. The items you share are engaged with for a long time. YouTube probably has the advantage in this category because it is less focused on real-time sharing.

- **Virality.** Because YouTube has more functionality related to embedding and sharing content outside of YouTube, it probably has an advantage over Instagram when it comes to overall virality. That being said, the simplicity of liking an Instagram image allows it to be socially shared very quickly and very broadly within the Instagram platform. In that regard, Instagram gets the nod. Instagram also allows for easy sharing onto Facebook. It is not unrealistic to think that it will also develop easy image sharing with Pinterest in the future. In 2012, Instagram and Twitter started to have a feud that has impacted sharing functionality between the two. This is likely a long-term situation, as both companies realize that they are in an intense competition for users.

Instagram Compared with Pinterest

Instagram and Pinterest were the two breakout stars of 2012. While the sites are similar in many ways, the biggest difference is that Instagram was built as a photo editing and sharing app, while Pinterest was built as a traditional website to "share the things you love." Instagram features images almost exclusively, whereas Pinterest features infographics, memes, how-to graphics, videos, audio clips, and even slide shows.

The other primary difference is the referral link system inherent in Pinterest. In my previous book, *Pinterest Power,* we chronicled the amazing power of Pinterest to generate referral links. While Instagram doesn't have this type of system, it does have one huge advantage. It is built for mobile use. When it comes to comparing them for marketing purposes, a few key differences emerge:

- **Time and energy required.** Both can be very efficiently managed and yet can consume a huge amount of time if you let them. There is no reason you cannot see good success by spending 10 to 20 minutes on each site daily.

- **Follower expectations.** Both sites are social media "lite" and don't require as much social interaction as Facebook or Twitter. The primary social engagement on Instagram is to like an image, with the secondary social engagement being to leave a comment. On Pinterest, the primary social engagement is to repin the item, with the secondary social engagement being the like. Each of these behaviors is accomplished very quickly on both sites.

- **Half-life of the content.** Content on both sites has a fairly long useful existence. The nod probably goes to Pinterest in this category, as the pinboard methodology serves as a helpful way to keep and share things for a very long time.

- **Virality.** It is common to share an item on Instagram and have it receive dozens of likes in a few moments. It is very rare for that to occur on Pinterest. However, the content on Pinterest continues to be liked and commented on for weeks and even months, so over time the amount of engagement on items is probably similar.

Instagram Compared with Twitter

Instagram and Twitter appear to be in a bitter feud, and they want users to decide between them. In late 2012, Instagram blocked its images from working inside the Twitter timeline, and Twitter launched its own photo filter functionality to compete directly with what users can do on Instagram. The feud has only been aggravated by the fact that in August 2012, less than two years after being founded, Instagram surpassed Twitter in terms of daily active users.

Of all the social networks, these two seem to be the most similar in terms of the core user behavior. We'll talk more about that in Chapter 5. The primary reason they behave so similarly is that the primary user behavior on both of them is to follow people.

When it comes to comparing them for marketing purposes, a few key differences emerge when we look at our factors:

- **Time and energy required.** Social sharing on Instagram is as simple as snapping a picture and uploading it. Sure, you can add a message and other details to make it more meaningful, but you don't have to. The Instagram model is not based on real-time sharing as much as the Twitter model, but it is part of the social norm. Because Twitter comes with the expectation of participating in conversations and conducting real-time sharing, and Instagram doesn't have those features as part of its social norm, the nod goes to Instagram.

- **Follower expectations.** The primary social action on both Twitter and Instagram is to follow someone. That is the method of voting and showing your support for someone's work. Twitter followers expect real-time sharing, comments, and responses. Instagram followers expect you to post pictures, which is simpler than having conversations. So the advantage clearly goes to Instagram in this case.

- **Half-life of the content.** A tweet has a social half-life of just a few minutes. A picture shared on Instagram has a much longer useful life. This becomes even more true when you consider the website version of Instagram profiles and how images are displayed for easy viewing.

- **Virality.** Retweeting does occur, but I don't think most people would consider it common for the average user, with the exception of celebrities or gurus. It is incredibly uncommon for a tweet to go viral. Social sharing on Instagram occurs when an image is liked, and this can frequently occur thousands of times within a few minutes.

A Basic Marketing Plan for Instagram

There are lots of tactics to advance your cause within Instagram, but if you don't have a basic marketing strategy outlined, you run the risk of aimlessly going from activity to activity without a clear direction. The following marketing strategy is the one we are using at Liberty Jane Clothing. It works well for physical product sellers, digital product sellers, service providers, and even nonprofits.

We first pioneered this marketing plan when we launched our Pinterest account. The marketing strategy is easy to follow and allows your account to grow rapidly. When we launched this strategy on Pinterest, it allowed us to get over 5,000 followers in our first year on the site. It is proving to be just as effective on Instagram. The steps are as follows.

The Anchor

The first step in a solid marketing plan on Instagram has to be a well-crafted profile. A profile that has authority and credibility is important.

Your profile lets existing customers as well as prospective customers know what you're using Instagram for and what they can expect.

The most basic choice is whether to use a corporate or brand name for your profile or whether to use your personal name. In our case at Liberty Jane Clothing, we decided using our brand name was appropriate. In some situations, a company will have a spokesperson who will use his or her personal profile to represent the company. Whatever you decide, it is important to make it clear to current and prospective customers.

The written description and profile picture are your tools for building a strong profile. The profile description allows for 150 characters. That's a very short space to clarify who you are. Ideally, a powerful profile will have the following attributes:

- A professional headshot or nicely formatted corporate logo

- A welcoming greeting

- A clear statement about your role in the company

- A clear statement about what the company does

- A credibility indicator, if you have one you can briefly share

- A description of the types of images you'll share

- A call to action, such as "Follow along!"

- A link to your most appropriate website

The Offer

Your absolute best launch strategy is having your existing customers find and follow you on Instagram. Why? They will find and follow their friends when they create an Instagram account, and then they will find and follow you. When they like your images, their friends will be exposed to your brand.

Instagram reportedly has over 100 million users. But even with that number of existing users, there will undoubtedly be a huge number of your current customers that have not heard about the app or not taken the time to download it and set up an account. You want to be the one to invite them to try out the app and begin following you.

The Visual Curator

Your image strategy is a vital part of your success. If there is one strategic issue to resolve when creating an Instagram marketing plan it is, *What is our image-sharing strategy?* You want to become a visual curator for your followers, sharing things that you think they will appreciate. Your image strategy, if well conceived, will allow you to develop consistent behavior over time, which instills confidence in your followers. Conventional wisdom says that you should take a quality-over-quantity approach to your image sharing on Instagram. But you'll have to decide what that means for your situation and whether it is the right approach for your followers. What defines quality photography in your niche or industry? You'll want to consider:

- How frequently should you share images?

- What types of images are you going to focus on?

- What times of the day or night are you going to share images?

- Are there quality or editorial standards you are going to impose on your work?

- Who gets to post images, who approves them, and who implements the overall long-term plan?

Chemical X

There is likely a reason your Instagram followers will start following you. To point out the obvious—they saw something in your profile that they liked, and they want to see more of it. Do you know what it is? It might be one of the following concepts:

- **An insider's view of your company.** Showing your followers a behind-the-scenes look at how you do things is sometimes very appealing.

- **A view of your private life.** If your followers idolize you, then they will likely appreciate seeing you living an exciting life.

■ **A preview of upcoming products or projects.** A sneak peek is an easy way to engage mentally and emotionally with your customers.

Now that we have identified a basic marketing strategy for Instagram, we can begin to focus on how best to position your brand on Instagram; then we will focus on a collection of specific monetization strategies.

THE SNAPSHOT

(1) Use the 5-10-20 test to determine if you need to use social media. (2) Learn how Instagram works compared with other social media sites and decide how it can fit into your strategy. (3) Create your four-step Instagram marketing plan and roll it out quickly. (4) Make sure your marketing strategy serves your customers and prospects with relevant images, not randomness.

The Social Network Hiding Inside Instagram

In addition to being a great photo filter app, Instagram provides a social sharing system that is very easy to use and really engaging. It is almost too easy to overlook the power of the social network that is hiding inside Instagram because of the beauty of the images and the simplicity of the system. But that would be a mistake. As marketers, we want to understand everything we can about how the social networking aspect of Instagram works so that we can leverage the platform for maximum impact.

As with Pinterest, Instagram is "social media lite," meaning that the culture is not very conversational and no one expects you to do much talking. The social network is technically built on a real-time sharing concept, because users share images in a timeline-based system. However, the content users' share is not as short-lived as a Twitter tweet or a Facebook post. Instagram images are appreciated for a very long time. Even though the conversations are less frequent, there is a culture of sharing and engagement that has real power.

The social sharing elements of Instagram are really the basis for our marketing plan. As with all other social networks, the primary question any marketer should ask is, *How can I serve my community of current and future customers effectively on this site?* Your aim and ambition must be subordinated to the aspirations and goals of your clientele. In simple terms, it is not about you. You get rewarded when you give your followers what they want.

As we mentioned in Chapter 4, Instagram is a lot like Twitter when it comes to the social aspects of the site. Why is Instagram similar to Twitter in terms of social behavior? There are three primary reasons:

1. Twitter and Instagram are both based on real-time sharing. Because you can post old images on Instagram, there is less emphasis on real-time activity than on Twitter. There is even a social norm on Instagram referred to in hashtags as tbt, or Throwback Thursday, when users deliberately share older images on Thursday. This tbt phenomenon suggests that real-time sharing is what people generally expect. That being said, I have not found this social convention to be overly strong, but you shouldn't be afraid to post old images if they are good.

2. Following people is the primary social behavior on both sites. It could be argued that liking an image is the primary social behavior on Instagram, but following someone is also a very common behavior.

3. Your number of followers is a social status issue. On both sites, when a user decides to follow someone, it is akin to casting a vote of approval.

The Power of an Invitation

Asking your existing fans and followers to join you on Instagram is the first step in building your profile. You can easily invite your existing Facebook contacts, but if you are trying to build a business profile, then your existing Facebook contacts may or may not be the right group to start with.

A better strategy is to begin introducing your Instagram work to your existing customers, fans, and followers. Including a call to action to follow you on Instagram is a great way to launch your Instagram effort. The challenge, of course, is that you cannot have people click from their computer screen to the App Store to download the Instagram app. They have to pick up their phone to complete the process. So your call to action can take one of two forms.

Your call to action can drive them to visit your Instagram web page, such as http://instagram.com/libertyjaneclothing. If they are already Instagram users, they can log in and begin following you. They do not need to interact with their phones to complete this process. When they go to their Instagram app on their phones, your images will begin showing up in their feeds. Another approach is to simply recommend that they download the Instagram app on their phones and begin following you. This is a weaker call to action and is probably less ideal than the first method.

For reasons I outlined in Chapter 4, it is vital to be part of your customers' onboarding process for Instagram. If you help them join and orient them to the site, then you have a huge starting advantage for meeting new prospective customers.

But Why Should I Help Instagram Grow?

You might be thinking, *Hey, wait a minute. I wanted to get traffic out of Instagram so I could grow my business. I don't want to send traffic to Instagram to grow its business.* Why should you start inviting your existing customers to discover and enjoy Instagram? Why would you take the time and energy to promote the company? In a word—*bonding*. Consider the results of your existing customers joining Instagram based on your recommendation:

- You've gotten them to act on your recommendation, which is a step toward becoming a trusted advisor.

- You've recommended something to them that they didn't know about, and in that way, you have positioned yourself as hip.

- You've given them a new way to like your products, by literally liking them on Instagram.

- You've given them a new way to support your brand and show their enthusiasm for your work.

- You've given them a way to introduce you to their friends. Each time they find a new friend on Instagram and begin being followed, your network of social sharing expands.

- You've created an alternative platform to connect on, strengthening your fans' methods of staying connected to your company.

Perfect People to Follow

So how do you identify the right people to follow on Instagram? And how do you get the right people to follow you? Let's look at two key groups:

Key Group One

Let's say 100 of your existing customers join Instagram, and they begin following you. Let's say that each of them has 25 followers, and they also follow a different group of 25 people. When you add it all up, that is 5,000 people who you know are associated with your current customers. You can literally see these people's profiles and their Instagram images if you simply take the time to look at the lists.

It stands to reason that this group would make great prospects. They are the perfect people to pursue, the friends of your current customers. Imagine the social impact if all 5,000 followed you. In fact, it is far wiser to build a following made up of very interested prospects than it is a following of random people. So your social behavior needs to be intentional and targeted. Don't just start following people because they have pretty pictures. Follow people who are good prospects.

But there is just one problem. If you follow 5,000 people but only have 100 followers, you will look like a spammer. You don't want to look like a spammer, and controlling the number of people you follow versus the number of people following you is a vital part of managing that perception.

So you need to be smart about how you pursue the 5,000 prospective customers. Over time, what you'll realize is that posting images is just one part of the marketing effort. The second part, and probably more important part, is the ongoing activity of following, liking, and commenting. To pursue your 5,000 prospects, there are several steps you can take.

The first step you can take is to begin following them in small batches of 40 to 50. By following them in batches and waiting a few days, you'll see who follows you back. If they follow you back, then you should consider them interested in you, your products, or your company. Or at least consider them favorably inclined toward the images you've shared in your feed and the description you've created for your profile. This is generally referred to on Twitter as a follow-to-be-followed strategy, and it works very well on Instagram.

After you determine if these people are going to follow you or not, you can unfollow the people who didn't follow you; and in that way, you can keep the overall number of people you're following fairly similar to the number of people following you. Then you simply "rinse and repeat."

A second and third step you can take is to begin liking and commenting on their images. These are substantial strategies, so let's cover them both in greater detail later in this chapter.

Key Group Two

There is a second group of people who are ideal to follow and whom you want to have following you. You can apply this same small-batch strategy to this group, and it is plausible that the people in this group will respond even more favorably than the first group. You probably already know the people I'm talking about—they are the ones using the hashtags associated with your industry, niche, or product.

Let's look at a specific example: Dakota Mechanic Studios. Dakota Mechanic Studios is an artisan workshop. Brian Lites, the founder, takes World War II–era airplane parts and turns them into functional art, like bookends and clocks. He sells the items at auction on eBay and does well. His social media marketing includes working with Pinterest and Instagram. Figure 5.1 presents an image he recently shared. Notice in the figure the industry-specific hashtags Brian uses when he publishes his images. They include #avion, #avgeek, #aircraft, #airplane, #aviation, #airplanes, #airplane_lovers, #pratt, #plane, and #warbird.

Brian uses general hashtags as well. They include #favorite, #popular, #igers, #igdaily, #instago, #instagood, #instagram, #instamood, #instagrammer, #instagrammers, #webstagram, and #clock. Is this too many hashtags? It might be, but ultimately it is up to each user to decide how many is too many. In this case, because half are targeted at Brian's industry, there is a good rationale for using so many.

Figure 5.1 An image from Dakota Mechanic Studios that includes industry-specific hashtags

Each of these industry-specific hashtags will have a specific group of people who use them. Those people are great prospects for Brian's airplane art. Let's choose one of these hashtags to look at more closely— #avgeek. If you look on the Instagram Explorer tab and search for the hashtag #avgeek, you'll notice that over 60,000 images use that hashtag. That's a huge collection. It stands to reason that if Brian begins following the people who are posting those pictures, they'll follow him back, and they'll begin to be exposed to his products.

While we're looking at Brian's Instagram image, we should probably point out three other marketing-related elements. First, he has embedded his logo on the image as a form of branding. We'll talk more about this in Chapter 7. Second, he has included a very clear sales message in the image description: "This is my last Pratt & Whitney R-2800 master rod clock. Up for auction on Ebay." Notice that he uses scarcity and urgency in his message. We will talk more about writing effective messages for Instagram in Chapter 11.

Notice that Brian's image has 28 likes and even a nice compliment that says, "Now that is cool!" You've got to appreciate the positive energy and goodwill created by that type of response. These people have seen an advertisement on Instagram and have liked it. Who says you can't advertise on Instagram? We'll talk about advertising in greater detail in Chapter 11.

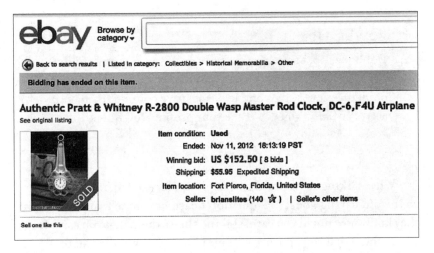

Figure 5.2 The Dakota Mechanic Studios clock image after it was sold on eBay

You may be wondering how Brian's auction ended. His master rod clock ended up selling for $152.50. He had eight people bidding to win the item. His auction was viewed 296 times. Figure 5.2 shows his eBay listing.

Can we attribute this result to Instagram directly? No, but we can say that at least 28 people saw and liked the item on Instagram before the auction ended. The actual number of viewers was probably much higher.

Liking Images

There is another great way to reach out to your circle of 5,000 prospects. You can like their pictures. Liking images is the fastest and easiest way to get noticed by prospective customers. Simply like a few of their photos, and they'll notice you. It's like introducing yourself in a friendly way. If you want to grow your followership very quickly, begin liking tons of images. Don't underestimate the power of simply liking people's pictures. You will add hundreds if not thousands of followers if you faithfully like pictures every day.

The nice part about liking people's images is that it will get you noticed, but it does not have the negative consequences associated with following a lot of people. In other words, people won't accuse you of being a spammer if you simply like 200 pictures a day.

POWER TIP

Don't just post a picture and wait for people to start following you. Make it your goal to follow good prospects, like lots of pictures every day, and leave positive comments. Be proactive socially, and you'll see your profile grow quickly.

Why is liking so important? People are focused on themselves, and as the old saying goes, "People don't care how much you know until they know how much you care." Liking shows them that you care. It also shows them that you approve of their photography skills and their profile. Liking makes people feel good about their Instagram work.

An easy way to quickly like an image is to simply double tap on it. This functionality works nicely in the Instagram app. Unfortunately, there is no equivalent on the website version. On the website, you must click on the image and then click the Like button.

Leaving Comments

Another terrific way to get noticed by your target audience is to simply comment on one of their pictures. Leave a sincere compliment, ask a question about the picture, or make a statement related to the picture. This behavior is not unwelcome on Instagram, and if you're being sincere, it is a fantastic way to get your name in front of a lot of people. Not only will the person who owns the image notice you, but the person's friends who like the image will also see your comment and take notice.

As with the follow-to-be-followed strategy, you want to be very intentional about the images you are leaving comments on. You want to deliberately focus on people who are either following your current followers or using a niche or industry hashtag. There is no bigger waste of time than leaving random comments on images in Instagram. Be focused, be intentional, and be sincere.

Of course, you'll also want to respond to comments that people leave on your images. To respond quickly, simply hit Comment and then tap the person's comment (see Figure 5.3). You'll notice a gray slider that allows you to either type a reply or hit the Delete key. In this way you can leave a quick reply or quickly deal with spam comments.

Figure 5.3 Responding to a comment is quick when you simply tap the person's comment.

Social Goals to Consider

A laser works because it is focused. Your social media strategy on Instagram needs to have a laserlike focus. If you want to grow your profile aggressively, make it your practice to do the following activities on Instagram each day:

- Post two to three pictures.

- Follow 40 people.

- Like 100 pictures.

- Unfollow 20 people who are not following you.

Antisocial on Instagram

People frequently ask us how we've gotten over 9,000 followers on You-Tube. Many Fortune 500 brands don't have 9,000 subscribers on YouTube, but our tiny company does. We tell them that we treat it like a social network, not just a video-hosting platform. It sounds simple, but you'd be surprised at how many marketers make that mistake. They just post content without creatively finding and engaging with their ideal prospects. The same principle applies to Instagram.

If you simply use Instagram as a photo-hosting platform and don't take the time to use the social media aspects of the site, then you'll run the risk of having very anemic results. You've got to be social. The best possible use of Instagram is to engage with your tribe in a relational way. That means following people, liking pictures, and commenting.

THE SNAPSHOT

(1) Instagram is not conversationally intensive, but it still requires social actions. (2) Learn methods for identifying and following good prospects. (3) Create activity goals for yourself so you can be proactive about connecting socially. (4) Never fall into the habit of just posting pictures without engaging socially.

Catalysts for Growth

When you start building your Instagram profile, you'll have zero followers on day one. That's an embarrassing place to be for a proud brand manager. Everyone has to go from zero to 10, then 10 to 100, before they can go from 100 to 1,000 and so on. You want to accelerate your growth as quickly as possible so that people see your work on the social network as impressive.

You want to grow as quickly as possible up to a level that most people would consider respectable. That number will be different for different people and brands, but for a small business, having 1,000 fans or more seems like a minimum acceptable standard. You'll probably wonder how many Instagram followers I have as the writer of this book. There is a number somewhere in the back of your mind that you consider a reasonable number, and when you see how many followers I have, you will think, *Okay, this guy is legit,* if I meet that expectation. Feel free to look up my profile and see if your expectations are met. My Instagram user name is @mrjasonmiles; or via the website, go to http://www.instagram.com/mrjasonmiles. Our business account is http://www.instagram.com/libertyjaneclothing.

POWER TIP

If you're a small-business owner, work hard to get 1,000 Instagram followers as quickly as you can. Everyone has to start somewhere, but with 1,000 fans or more, you generally will be seen as having a relevant profile. If you manage a larger brand, then obviously this number should be higher.

Coca-Cola, of course, will have a different number, as its threshold of legitimacy is much higher. We expect more from Coca-Cola because we know it is one of the world's biggest brands.

At Liberty Jane Clothing, we always have the same goal when we launch on a new social media platform. We aim to get to 1,000 followers as quickly as possible. For us, that's the number that indicates credibility. We can only speculate about whether that number meets our customer's expectations, but that is how we approach the start-up effort. You can look up our business profile and see how we're doing by going to @libertyjane or by going to the website at http://www.instagram.com/libertyjaneclothing. I would encourage you to establish a similar initial goal to get 1,000 followers as quickly as you can.

Have you ever looked at a company's social media profile and felt underimpressed by the number of followers it has? You can see this most frequently on YouTube, where even massive companies have a very difficult time getting people to subscribe to their channels. There are several brands and guru-type people that immediately come to mind as I'm writing this, which I could include as examples, but I don't want to embarrass them publicly. These big underachievers have massive advertising budgets, whole armies of marketers, and ad agencies to back them up, but they can't get more than a few hundred subscribers on YouTube. But tiny companies, or even more embarrassing, seventh graders in their bedrooms, can get tens of thousands of followers and millions of video views. Like it or not, the number of followers you have is one of the primary methods by which people verify credibility.

The sad truth is paradoxical: people will follow popular people (or brands) more easily than they will unpopular people (or brands). This can create something I call the "failure to socially thrive syndrome." You launch your profile and it languishes. You have to actively manage your way through this condition by taking deliberate action.

There are specific actions that you can take that serve as catalysts for growth. You want to use all the legitimate catalysts for growth that you can. Novice social media marketers assume that "organic growth" means "unadded growth," but this is not true.

The truth is, there are things that won't and don't happen unless something else happens first. This is the basic concept of a catalyst. Popcorn will never pop unless you heat it up, and your Instagram profile will never aggressively grow unless you use a proper catalyst. Setting up a profile and doing the basic user behaviors, in this case uploading pictures, will not create a flash mob of organic growth. That's not a realistic amount of effort, no matter how good your pictures are.

Let's look at five catalysts for organic growth and see if they apply to your situation. Scientists define catalysts in two broad groups: positive catalysts and negative catalysts. Positive catalysts speed things up, while negative catalysts slow things down. Another term for negative catalysts is *inhibitors*. First, we'll look at three positive catalysts and then two negative ones.

Catalyst #1 (Positive). A New Service for Existing Customers

As we outlined in Chapter 4, one of the primary action steps of a basic marketing plan is inviting your existing fans, followers, and friends to follow you on Instagram. The larger your social reach on other platforms, the faster you'll be able to catalyze growth on Instagram past your initial goal.

Let's look at an example. The amazing Money Saving Mom blog, as seen in Figure 6.1, is a website that serves a very large community of home economists.

At the time of this writing, the site has the following metrics:

- **Facebook followers.** 211,749

- **Twitter followers.** 99,235

- **YouTube subscribers.** 1,606 (583,555 video views)

- **Pinterest followers.** 23,359

Figure 6.1 Money Saving Mom's website and social media reach constitute a significant platform.

- **Newsletter subscribers.** Unknown but probably well over 100,000

- **Unique monthly website visitors.** 750,000

- **Monthly website page views.** Over 4 million

Her new Instagram account will start with zero followers, but imagine how quickly it will grow if she positions it as an exciting new way to see what she's up to. You can see how she's doing at http://instagram .com/crystalpaine .

Each business is different, but everyone has some social reach, even if a person is just starting out. In Chapter 5, we outlined why tapping into this existing base of users is a wise idea. In order to fully leverage this strategy, you need to answer one question for your existing customers: *Why should I follow you on Instagram if I already follow you on Twitter* (or *Facebook* or *Pinterest*)? The answer to that question is what you might call your "Instagram value proposition."

You want to position your Instagram account as a new service for your existing customers. Here is how we are doing this at Liberty Jane Clothing as it's related to our other social assets:

- **Facebook.** General news and conversations

- **Pinterest.** Our collection of "things we love"

- **YouTube.** Contests and how-to videos

- **Newsletter.** A weekly recap of our new product offerings

- **Instagram.** Behind-the-scenes images of our work and life

Maybe you'll use Instagram for something else, but for us, this is the most logical use and what informs our value proposition. This value proposition guides us as we share images. We are also repeating this message to our fans, followers, and friends via our existing platforms. In Part 5 of this book, we'll explain in greater detail how to integrate Instagram with your other social assets.

Catalyst #2 (Positive). Social Action

As we outlined in Chapter 5, using the basic social behaviors on Instagram will help build up your number of followers. These behaviors are not complicated, but they do take a lot of time. They are the basic social actions. These include:

- Liking other users' images within your niche

- Following other users within your niche

- Commenting on other users' images within your niche

- Responding to comments that people have made on your images

There is one factor that directly affects your ability to use these actions to grow your number of followers, and that is simply the amount of time you spend on Instagram conducting social actions. There might be shortcuts, but this is a tried-and-true method.

It's important to distinguish between uploading pictures and the other social actions we outlined in Chapter 5 and engaging in the more relational social actions at this point. As we've discussed previously, it is better to upload fewer high-quality images than many poorer-quality images.

Let's assume that hypothetically it takes five minutes of Instagram work to get one new follower. You can spend that time liking images, making comments, or following new people. Whatever you do, it needs to be strategic engagement, not random activity. It stands to reason that if you increase your time on the site by a factor of 10 (50 minutes a day on the site), then the number of followers will increase by a factor of 10 (10 followers a day). At that rate, it would take you 100 days, or just over 3 months of working 50 minutes a day, to reach your goal of 1,000 followers. How can you improve that result? Here are a few suggestions:

- Follow people in your niche who have roughly the same number of followers as people they are following. In other words, avoid people who have a very large following but who don't follow very many people. They simply won't follow you back, nor will they notice that you started following them.

- After you start following people, start liking their images regularly so they see you in their News Feed tab. That will improve the odds that they will notice you and follow you back.

- Like recent images. When an image is uploaded to Instagram, the first few likers get their user names displayed underneath the image. But beyond 10 likers, it simply says "11 likes," and the names are concealed. So liking an image immediately after it is uploaded allows your user name to be displayed on the image until more than 10 people like it.

- Follow the people who liked your product images. These are people who have endorsed your product—you really ought to like them!

- Leave comments frequently on many people's images. It seems that likes are so common on Instagram that they don't necessarily help you stand out as much as a comment does. So provide nice comments.

Catalyst #3 (Positive). High-Quality Images

Mastering Catalyst #2 will get you noticed, but if you want someone to start following you, your profile presentation and your images need to be good. The topic of picture quality should probably get an entire chapter, but there are many books and resources online that can help you improve your photography. Plus I'm a marketer, not a photographer, so I'll share what I know and recommend that you seek further help as needed. Let's review a few of the basic concepts briefly:

- **Composition.** The composition or layout of the image can radically change how people perceive it. The same scene can result in an amazing picture or a boring one, depending on how the photographer arranges the visual elements.

- **Lighting.** Your lighting will be different for product photography versus other types of photography. Mastering lighting is one of the keys to effective photography. Most commonly, natural light produces a nicer result than indoor lighting.

- **Subject matter.** Having an interesting subject is the most important part of any photo. The biggest challenge most photographers face is trying to identify interesting subject matter.

- **Simplicity.** Many times, photographs are made more interesting by what is left out, rather than what is included. Cropping out irrelevant elements and allowing the viewer to focus on just one aspect of the scene will improve most images.

- **Focal point.** Having a single focal point is part of striving for simplicity. The question for every image is, *What will people be drawn toward within the image, and how can I prominently position that part?*

- **Perspective.** You have the opportunity to tell a story with your images. Your perspective is unique, and the way you take the photo reflects that uniqueness. For example, when you're standing in an orchard, you can focus on the strict order of the tree planting, the leaves or bark on the tree, or a bird on a branch. Each is a different perspective on the same orchard.

- **Point of view.** The angle at which you take a picture can affect the final result dramatically. Many times, simply raising the camera up higher or kneeling down can change the point of view enough to move an image from boring to interesting.

- **Filters.** Instagram was designed to allow iPhone photographers to edit and share their images. The filters included in the app allow you to substantially alter your photos. How you do that can either make them look brilliant and inviting or cause them to look "off" and "wrong." Over time, you'll come to use different filters for different situations.

- **Black and white versus color.** One of the simplest ways to increase the interest in a photo is by making it black and white instead of color. Instagram has several filters that allow you to do different versions of black and white.

- **Unedited or filtered.** There is a "purist" tribe of users within Instagram that has a real disdain for filters. They would much rather see images that are high quality and unedited than lower quality and edited heavily. You'll have to choose which perspective you want to take on.

- **Sharpness.** Most mobile phones allow you to focus on several areas on the screen before you take the picture, and by doing so you can alter the sharpness of the focal point or make things intentionally less sharp.

- **Depth of field.** A common technique in portrait and product photography is the concept of a shallow depth of field—having the focal point in your image be closer to the camera and in focus and having the background be intentionally unfocused. While smartphone cameras cannot create this effect out of the box, as you might guess, there's an app for that! Try SynthCam for the iPhone.

- **Color saturation.** A common issue with images is that they are not as vibrant as they could be. The Photoshop Express app helps you resolve this issue and many other common issues mentioned in this section.

Catalyst #4 (Negative). Bad Profile Presentation

Having a profile that frightens people is a bad move. Social media is filled with creepers—bots, spammers, and whackos—and you don't want people to wonder if you fall into one of those categories. There are specific things to avoid to ensure you don't fall into any of those categories, including:

- **Using an odd profile name that doesn't make it clear who you are and what you're about.** This can be a challenge if your business name is long. If you're an expert or public figure operating in your niche under your user name, it's sometimes a challenge to clarify the connection with your brand or company. But you should strive to have a clear and easy-to-understand name.

- **Not distinguishing between your profile name and your name.** It is also important to note that your profile name is one piece of information, and Instagram allows you to have a name that can be different. I realize it's confusing, but your profile name and your name are two different things, which you can use to clarify who you are. Your profile name forms your Instagram account user information, @mrjasonmiles, and the basis for your website URL, http://www.instagram.com/mrjasonmiles. Your name shows up in the Instagram app immediately under your profile name, and on the website form it shows up immediately before your biography. So if you are wise about using both together, you can clarify who you are using a combination of both.

- **Leaving weird comments.** Your comments should be kind and friendly, but not weird. There are a million ways to make a weird comment, but it would certainly include messages that don't make sense or are too personal.

- **Liking personal images.** Although not directly related to profile presentation, another negative catalyst is liking people's personal images. If people share 50 images of lakes, sunsets, and flowers, along with four of themselves with their friends, like the flowers, not the friends. Liking personal images makes you seem like a creeper. Liking people's good nonpersonal images suggests that you like their photography skills, which is not creepy.

Catalyst #5 (Negative). Poorly Chosen Images

As we talked about in Chapter 4, your image strategy is a critical part of your success on Instagram. There are lots of ways to damage your user experience and follower growth by choosing images poorly. Let's review a few commonsense ideas:

- **Choose images that will resonate with your target market.** If you are trying to cultivate fans and followers to help promote your brand or product, then your images should be enjoyable to your followers. This requires a bit of customer research and thoughtful analysis.

- **Choose images that are high quality.** This is a no-brainer. Your images need to be really good. Sometimes the quality of an image is in the eye of the beholder, but many times the image quality is a direct reflection of the primary photography skills involved. It is better to leave out mediocre photos and have fewer overall images than to include them.

- **Choose images that will not offend anyone.** Most corporate marketers have the discipline, or fear of being fired, that prevents them from including questionable images. But sadly, many bloggers and online marketers have not considered how damaging inappropriate content can be to their brand.

THE SNAPSHOT

(1) Everybody has to start with no followers, but work through that quickly by using Instagram to add value for existing customers. (2) Determine to get 1,000 followers as quickly as you can. (3) Spend your time strategically engaging with the right prospects, not just random people. (4) Watch out for negative catalysts for growth and avoid them.

A Copywriter Walks into the App Store

Although Instagram is an app for editing and sharing images, you still get to do a substantial amount of copywriting. That's great news for those of us trying to promote our brands. As marketers, the challenge of combining words and images will feel very familiar to us. Display advertising is made up of these component parts. It is the skillful use of words and images woven together to tell an interesting story about your product or brand. Yes, we get to do that on Instagram.

In Chapter 11, we'll dive deeply into how to use Instagram for display advertising campaigns. Don't worry; we are going to master the art of tasteful display advertising on Instagram, not the lame, spammy type of advertising that you might have run into on the app. But before we can do that, we need to understand all the ways in which we can include writing on Instagram.

We also need to ask a hard question: *What would a genius copywriter do if he or she were crafting the written messages associated with an Instagram photo?* Someone like Joe Sugarman comes to mind. Joe is the author of the *Adweek Copywriting Handbook* and is famous for making millions from TV ads featuring BluBlocker Sunglasses. How would he use Instagram? Let's first look at the possible writing opportunities and then review how a legendary copywriter might use them.

Writing Opportunities on Instagram

You might be surprised at how many writing elements you can include as you share an Instagram image (see Figure 7.1). Let's review them together.

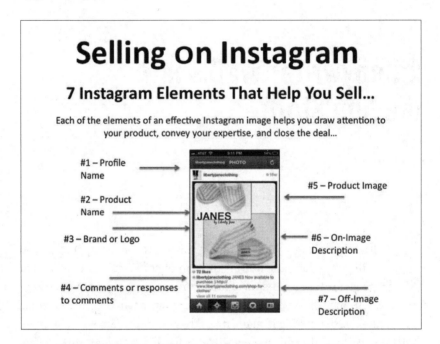

Figure 7.1 There are seven elements of an Instagram image that you can use to share a written message.

There are two broad categories of writing in Instagram: writing on the image itself and writing that is off the image. Part of the off-image information is referred to as metadata—the information that accompanies the image. But the other part should not be overlooked either, and that includes your profile details. Let's review both the off-image and on-image options.

Off-Image Elements

Smart marketers will use every element of the Instagram system as an opportunity to position their product for success. The strongest presentations will have a seamless flow of information from the off-image elements to the on-image elements. You can use the following off-image locations to share your message:

- **Profile name.** You'll have to decide whether to create an Instagram account for each brand or product line you manage or to create one account that serves your entire company. Obviously the choice will help inform your followers what you're all about. Most large companies that manage multiple brands typically have a unique social media account for each brand. That helps narrow the focus and ensure that you can work with one target market.

- **Comments or responses to comments.** You can add additional information in the comment section. As well, customers can comment, and you can provide additional information as a response.

- **Image caption.** The image caption or description is the primary location for your copywriting. This is where your inner J. Peterman can emerge if you're a product seller. If you're a service seller, this is where you want to position yourself or your service as a solution.

On-Image Elements

Your ability to write on Instagram doesn't stop at the edges of the image. Although the Instagram app's basic functionality doesn't allow you to write on the image, there are many ways to get around this limitation and bring words to life on the image. Once you figure out how to add information to your pictures, then the opportunities are endless to add descriptions, product names, price information, and other related sales copy. Let's look at a few of the most basic ways to enhance an image with copywriting:

- **Image descriptions or notes.** You can place an informational note or description on the image itself. Depending on the composition of the image, this can be easily added without detracting from the image's focal point. This can be achieved via third-party apps that we'll describe later in this book.

- **Logo or brand.** You'll have to decide how disciplined you want to be when it comes to adding a brand or logo to your images. In some cases, it makes perfect sense and should be considered. In other cases, it is an unnecessary hassle. Additionally, if you're trying to convey to your followers that you're taking behind-the-scenes shots, then placing a logo or brand mark on your image will not harmonize with that message.

- **Product name.** One aspect of on-image information that can be very helpful to your followers is adding the name of your product to the image. This is particularly true if you have many similar products, like jewelry, shoes, or dresses.

- **Pricing information.** According to the Shopify.com team, Pinterest pins with pricing information receive 36 percent more likes than pins without pricing information. Would that statistic hold true in Instagram? You'll have to test it to find out.

- **Launch date.** As we'll discuss in Chapter 13, Instagram is an ideal tool for product launches. One of the primary messages for that type of strategy is the announcement of when something will be available. While you can certainly include that information in the off-image description, you can also include it right on the image to reinforce the message.

- **Final sale date.** Scarcity is one of the buying triggers we'll discuss in Chapter 8. Including a message related to when the doors close or the product stops being sold is a terrific way to help people decide to buy.

How to Get Words on Your Pictures

So what are the best ways to add your messages to images? There are lots of options to choose from. Let's review the most common ways this can be accomplished:

- **Third-party apps.** The option to add messages onto your images via third-party apps is endless. These apps generally let you pick an image, write on it, and then save it to your camera's image library, where you can upload it to Instagram. Color Cap, for example, allows you to add text of various colors to an image, and instaCap allows you to add basic messages. There are many other options.

- **Photoshop Elements.** For more complex use of messages on images, you can use Photoshop Elements for the desktop. Don't worry; while the full version of Photoshop might intimidate you, the lighter and simpler Photoshop Elements is made for the novice user. The process for using Photoshop Elements would include editing the image in the program and then placing the image in your camera's library for use on Instagram. There are numerous ways to get an image into your phone's library, the easiest of which is probably to e-mail it to yourself and open the e-mail on your phone. But there are many other methods that work, too.

- **An image of an ad.** You can always simply take a picture of your previously created ad, but this will likely turn out poorly. But sometimes, if it is done in an attractive way, this type of shot can be effective.

- **A screenshot of an ad.** If you have your ad on your website and it looks the way you want it shared on Instagram, then your task is easy. Simply use your smartphone's web browser and visit your website. When you have the ad displayed on your phone's screen in the way you want, simply take a screenshot. It will take a picture of what you are looking at on your phone and add it to your phone's image library. To take a screenshot on an iPhone, simply press the Home and Sleep buttons at the same time. Screenshots on Android phones are possible, too. If you are using Android 4.0 (Ice Cream Sandwich) or a later version, then simply hold the Volume Down and Power buttons at the same time.

POWER TIP

Easily put the images from your website or Facebook photos into your phone's photo album by taking a screenshot of the images you want. Simply navigate to your website, look at the image, and on an iPhone press the Home and Sleep buttons at the same time. The image you're looking at will be saved as a picture in your photo album.

Common Myths

There are certainly challenges associated with copywriting for Instagram. Some are real constraints, and some are simply emotional resistance to doing the work, manifested in excuses or inaccurate assumptions. Let's debunk a few of these myths together.

Myth #1. There Isn't Enough Space to Add a Marketing Message

The truth is that all display advertisers are confronted with the challenge of limited space for words. Ever try to write an ad for the side of a bus? How about writing an ad for the top of a taxi? Space is limited in many formats. Dealing with constraints is just part of the creative exercise. In fact, the space restrictions help you hone your message and get very focused. My mantra is "Brevity, Clarity, Content, Style."

Myth #2. Ads Aren't Welcome on Instagram

This is a half-truth that nonmarketers generally wouldn't understand. The reality is that ads are very welcome on Instagram if they are matched to the right audience in the right way and solve a real problem. No one likes advertising when it is unwelcome, but that is like saying no one likes to hear a knock on the door during dinner. If the ad is a perfect solution to your urgent problem, it moves magically into a whole different category in your mind. Suddenly it is not an ad; it is a godsend. The ad becomes a serendipitous moment when your solution materialized just when you needed it most. The knock on the door during dinner isn't unwelcome if it's Publishers Clearing House.

Myth #3. I Will Do More Damage Than Good

If your Instagram followers are made up of your Facebook friends and coworkers, and you try to advertise to them for your new moonlighting career as a multilevel marketer, then you may very well be right. But Instagram won't be any more destructive than your personal e-mails would be or your unwanted "invitations to dinner." But if you target the right audience on Instagram and cultivate a followership of targeted prospects, then you will be solving problems, not damaging relationships.

Myth #4. Since I Don't Know How to Do Copywriting, I Better Not

If you're the marketer for your product or service, then you already know enough to make an effective presentation. Your only challenge is learning how to create effective copy. Luckily, we'll cover that in the next few paragraphs. The good news is that each Instagram image gives you another opportunity to practice this trade skill. Copywriters were not born or somehow ordained when they graduated with an English degree from a university. Copywriters are practitioners who start with a goal and never stop learning how to perfect their craft. You are a perfect candidate.

Myth #5. Social Media Isn't Good for Selling

Sadly, this myth is pervasive and is repeated regardless of which social media site you are talking about. At Liberty Jane Clothing, we use YouTube, Facebook, Pinterest, and Instagram to drive sales. Countless other companies use Twitter and Google+. Smart marketers are bonding with prospective customers and leading them through the sales cycle using social media. Don't believe the lie.

Myth #6. You Can't Include Hyperlinks, So Why Bother?

In my first book, I chronicled the amazing power of Pinterest to help marketers build a massive set of referral links within the site that all point toward your website. That puts Pinterest clearly in the category of an Internet marketing gold mine. Yet Instagram has its own strengths and acts much more like traditional offline display advertising. One day, Instagram might allow hyperlinks to be included in image captions. But until then, we can treat it like a fantastic mobile phone display ad system. Nothing wrong with that!

What Would Joe Sugarman Do?

No one would deny that copywriting has an artistic quality to it. But like most well-studied art, there are techniques that emerge over time to become the industry best practices. If you learn the best practices, then you are at least operating within the realm of possible quality. You may still stink at it, but your chances of getting it right improve if you learn the basic lessons.

The best copywriters are masters of technique that they effortlessly weave into their work over years of dedicated practice. They know why they are doing certain things and why they shouldn't do other things. The techniques absorb into their writing to such an extent that it looks intuitive to the outside observer. Thankfully, one of the masters, Joe Sugarman, has documented his work in a copywriting classic, *The Adweek Copywriting Handbook*. Study his work and learn to apply it to Instagram.

The Copywriter's Goal

Think back to a time when you were in a conversation on a topic that didn't interest you in any way. And to add insult to injury, the conversation was with someone you really didn't care to be around. I'd imagine you were trying to be polite, but you really couldn't wait to either change the subject or, ideally, walk away. Now think back to a conversation where someone told you a really exciting piece of gossip. Imagine that on top of it being an amazing piece of news, the person who shared it with you was someone you secretly admired very much and wanted to build a closer relationship with. I bet that you were emotionally engaged, eager to share your perspective, full of questions, and hopeful the conversation wouldn't stop and that you were smiling and generally hyper. In print and online advertising, the bored walk away—and if they decide they don't like you, they run away. Your job is to position yourself as an interesting person and your product as newsworthy.

If you have your target audience right, then the overall goal of your presentation is to structure the information in a "logical flow" (Sugarman, p. 97) that anticipates the question the viewer might ask next and answers that question. The goal is to start an interesting conversation in the mind of the prospect that the prospect is genuinely enthusiastic about finishing. The goal is getting the attention of the right people and leading them through the process of discovery.

The goal for each element of your presentation should be to strive for engagement with the prospect in this interesting conversation in an appealing way. You don't achieve success by being boring, annoying, or overly spammy in your approach. You achieve success by having a presentation that clicks with your target market and feels very natural, timely, and welcome. As we've outlined, the elements you get to use include the image, the on-image copy, the off-image copy, the metadata elements of your image, and the account-level information.

The Copywriter's View of the Basic Tools

Good copywriters integrate each aspect of the component parts available to create an overall environment. Each component does a job to help shape the environment. Let's look at each of the primary components related to an Instagram image and how a copywriter might consider using them:

1. **The profile name.** To describe who you are in a clear and compelling way. This is an exercise in creative branding that should resonate with your company, product, or personal brand.

2. **The name.** To give you more information and further explain who you are and what you're about. @libertyjaneco becomes Liberty Jane Clothing.

3. **The image.** This is the primary attention-getting device. It has one job to do—capture the attention of the ideal prospect. If it fails to capture the attention of the ideal prospect, nothing else matters.

4. **The on-image writing.** This information, such as a caption, product name, or price, is a critical part of explaining more about the product. It is likely the first written message the prospect will see. It must resonate well.

5. **The image caption.** This is the primary written message that interested prospects will read. It is critically important to continue the conversation and engage the reader by sharing information that helps the reader take the next logical step forward. Where is the item available? When does it go on sale or stop being sold? How much is it? Where can they read more information? The description does not need to sound like a sales pitch. It needs to offer answers to top-of-mind questions in a conversational tone.

6. **The comments.** You can immediately leave comments as if they are a "P.S." to offer a bit more information. Or you can wait until

someone asks a question. Either way, you have an opportunity to provide additional information about the product or service.

The Copywriter's Environment

The copywriter is creating an environment that proposes just one logical outcome—buying the product. But it happens in a set of steps. Every time the customer mentally says, *Yes, I like that—tell me more*, the copywriter has done his or her work in that part of the campaign. The overall mood is to have the prospect agree with your presentation, little by little, not in a sneaky or smarmy way, but in an exciting and logical way. The mood should be one of agreement.

On Instagram, that mood can be set. People's interest can be aroused, and their curiosity and enthusiasm can be sparked. The logical next step for selling is to clearly send them to the sales page or e-commerce site. If qualified, enthusiastic prospective buyers go from Instagram to the e-commerce site; then the Instagram marketer's job is done.

Taking Copywriting to the Next Level

In Chapter 8, we'll continue this conversation and learn about the emotional elements that help create a buying environment and how to include them in the Instagram marketing effort. Let's get started.

THE SNAPSHOT

(1) Copywriting can play a key part in your Instagram marketing work. (2) Evaluate how you can use the on-image and off-image areas to include your messages. (3) The goal of all good copywriting is to get the prospect to take the next logical step. (4) Avoid destructive myths about marketing on Instagram and learn to apply the principles of master copywriters like Joe Sugarman.

Part 3

BONDING AND BRANDING ON INSTAGRAM

Instant Buying Decisions on Instagram

Browse around on Instagram for a few weeks, and you'll notice an interesting trend. People like images that stir them emotionally: vacation destinations, sandy beaches, gourmet cuisine, sunsets, shoes, dresses, pretty places, and pretty faces. People aren't responding to the technical brilliance of an image; they want to be taken on an emotional ride. To see what really strikes a chord, observe people's comments. Look at the comments on the ModCloth image in Figure 8.1, for example.

Notice that the picture in Figure 8.1 was liked 13,200 times. There are 353 comments, including:

> "I just ordered it too! Hope it gets to me for New Years. :)"
>
> "I got it!"
>
> "I can't live without this."
>
> "I want!!"
>
> "Me too!"
>
> "Ah I want it! I just saw it on the site."

Notice that the comments center on the word *want*? There are powerful emotions at play when we see images on Instagram, just like there are when we see images on the Internet, on TV, in movies, or in

Figure 8.1 People react emotionally when they see something that excites them.

magazines. Images provoke thoughts and feelings that are the basis for buying decisions.

In this chapter, we'll dive into the concept of identifying and tapping into these deep-seated emotions and how you can weave them into your Instagram messages to call followers to action in effective ways. If you apply even a hint of these factors in the right way, then positive results will accrue from your work. In some ways, they are like perfume (or cologne)—there is an art to application that makes it not too faint and not too strong.

12 Common Buying Triggers Found on Instagram

There are dozens of emotional triggers that marketers have discovered since direct response marketing began. If you use them in your work, you'll prompt people to act. If you ever have a chance to look at a 1905 Sears Wish Book, a masterpiece of emotional selling, you'll immediately notice the strong use of these types of concepts in the images and copywriting. Instagram provides a new outlet for this age-old method.

For the sake of brevity, let's focus on 12 of the triggers that seem to be particularly prominent in Instagram marketing efforts. These emotional triggers are not mystical, fringe, or quack concepts. Nor are they difficult to figure out. They are completely obvious when you stop to look for them. The challenge for marketers is how to weave them into the story of your product or service in a way that is authentic, honest, and nonmanipulative. The trick is in the implementation. Let's review the 12 factors:

- **Love.** On Instagram, "Love" is a common reply to an image. The message is clear, isn't it? No other information is required. As marketers, we should strive to provide our followers with product images they can love. And if we're service providers, we need to consider how to share a message or concept that people will love. Of course, there is only one thing better than "Love," and that's "Love, Love, Love," which also seems to be a common response. People love places, food, clothing, puppies, and products. They love things they once had long ago, things they have right now, and things they want to get in the future. People are constantly loving something.

- **Desire.** Desire comes in many shapes and sizes. People have a deep desire to own things, to meet someone they find attractive, or to be noticed. Part of the sales process is instilling a sense of desire in a prospect, then building that to a higher level, and then helping the person find fulfillment by purchasing the item. We'll demonstrate how to use this trigger in an in-depth way in Chapter 13.

- **Involvement or ownership.** For most brands, the goal of customer engagement is to build a following of strong advocates that feel a personal involvement in and even ownership of the brand's success. These insiders feel so connected that they have adopted the goal of ensuring your brand is shared far and wide. By using Instagram to give a behind-the-scenes view, you have an opportunity to build a deeper level of involvement.

- **Justifying the purchase.** People need to rationalize a buying decision. People need to have an excuse in order to feel okay about what they've done. The excuse can come in many forms. A 24-hour sale provides an excuse. A coupon provides an excuse. A buy-one, get-one-free offer provides an excuse. A beautiful image of your product provides an excuse for them to like it and share it.

Building in a justification that gives prospective buyers an excuse is smart marketing, and it can certainly be done on Instagram.

- **Desire to belong.** For many smaller brands that create a sense of community, the desire to belong can be a powerful emotional trigger. People don't want to feel like they are missing a good party or being left out. Instagram provides a perfect platform to create a sense of belonging and participation.

- **Desire to collect.** Many people collect experiences. As an Instagram user, that is one of the primary activities you'll see being lived out. People collect travel experiences, exotic food experiences, hobby-related experiences, and friendships. People even work to collect followers on Instagram. Is there a way you can help your followers collect things?

- **Curiosity.** One of the strongest emotional triggers for Internet or direct response purchasing is the concept of curiosity. People want to know what the product is like, and they cannot experience it unless they order it. While in a retail environment a product can be picked up, tried on, and felt, in a virtual environment the only solution for strong curiosity is to order the item. Your images can either satisfy people's curiosity or fuel it. Present your items in a way that enhances the mystery and allure instead squelching it. For example, product images that are zoomed in provide incredible detail, and people immediately think, *I wonder what that fabric feels like?* Good product photography raises more questions than it answers.

- **Storytelling.** The opportunity to reveal a story and include people in a journey is a strong emotional trigger that is available for marketers using Instagram. In Chapter 13, we'll dive deeply into the use of this technique and explore how it can benefit your marketing efforts. Do you have a story to tell about your product or service? Can images on Instagram and the associated messages help position your story as intriguing, captivating, and fun?

- **Greed.** What motivates people to hunt for bargains and to swoop in quickly when they see a special deal? Greed is commonly the answer. Greed plays a big part in motivating people to act. Greed motivates people to enter contests, to show up early for a grand opening, and to stay up all night outside a store before a product launch.

- **Urgency.** Having a limited time to respond to an offer creates a sense of urgency. It is one of the best sales tools available. As a marketer, you can introduce a sense of urgency as you create display ads, or you can do it simply by explaining the details of a sale in an Instagram caption.

- **Instant gratification.** Retailers know that the impulse purchase is a key part of their sales opportunity. People want something immediately, and when they are in a buying mood, there is no stopping them. Instant gratification can certainly play a key role in driving consumer behavior on Instagram too. When a new product is launched, the buying mode sweeps over prospects, and they jump into action.

- **Exclusivity.** When something is rare, people inevitably want it more than when it is not. Featuring the rarity or uniqueness of an item tells people that if they want it, they are going to have to act quickly and not delay. They will feel a rush of pride for owning something that is uncommon. Many companies use this strategy intensively as they market items in limited edition sets, for a limited time, or as one-of-a-kind items.

Five Levels of Connection to a Message

Prospects will bond with your photography and messages at different levels. Sometimes you hit a home run—the emotional response to your work is intense and urgent, and a buying decision is easily prompted. Sometimes the level of emotion is not obvious, you only hit a single, and your target market responds mildly to your effort. Sometimes you strike out, and there is no emotional bond formed with your images and associated copywriting. When you do find some success, you are aided by other people's positive sentiments. If people start expressing a positive sentiment about your Instagram images, then you've got allies rallying to your side. You've got a tribe, and the members of your tribe are helping you deliver the message.

There are different levels of resonance you will have with an emotional trigger. Five immediately come to mind. Let's review them in order of weakest to strongest:

1. **You hear it from the company.** The positive sentiment is expressed in the item description or on the image in a way that makes it clear that the company is emotionally "up" about the item. You notice it, but the feeling doesn't transfer to you.

2. **You hear it from a third party.** Seeing a product photo on Instagram and noticing that other people are enthusiastic about it is a higher level of resonance. It is more authentic and powerful to see other people expressing their feelings about something. This is the level at which an Amazon book review resides, for example. This level is relatively easy to obtain on Instagram if you have a following of people who are enthusiastic about your niche or industry.

3. **You hear a weak recommendation from a person you know, like, or trust.** A personal mention of a product or service from someone you know is a fairly powerful emotional driver. This happens every day when people express a need. Someone will invariably try to be helpful and recommend a product or service, even if he or she hasn't personally tried it. Statements like "I heard so-and-so is pretty good" are common occurrences and provide emotional comfort on several levels. They allow the prospect to have an excuse to buy something, in addition to fueling curiosity.

4. **You say something privately about the company.** The level of emotional engagement goes up dramatically when you are the one expressing the positive sentiment. When you say, "I want that," even privately, your emotions are involved in a way that has a powerful effect on your long-term buying decision.

5. **You say it publicly.** When you are enthusiastic enough about a product or service to put it on your public wish list, then you are engaging emotionally on a very high level. On Instagram, you see people do this frequently, and their positive sentiment is encouraged, reinforced, and seconded by other people. When a group starts collectively saying, "We want this," a virtual frenzy occurs. Look again at the ModCloth image and the 13,200 likes and 353

comments and imagine what that would mean for your product or service.

Why You're Not Buying It

You've probably had an emotional reaction to this chapter. Either you liked it, or something about it made you feel uneasy. As you read it, either you thought of positive examples that reinforced what I was saying, or maybe you kept thinking of negative examples that highlighted how using emotion in the selling experience was wrong, mean, or manipulative. Your opinion about me and about this book may be on the line here. Fair enough.

If you're feeling uneasy about shaping people's emotional responses, then take a minute and look at the people who are the best in your industry. It really doesn't matter if you're a teacher, insurance salesman, car mechanic, or small retailer. I bet the best people in your industry weave emotion into their work. Do they shape people's emotional responses?

POWER TIP

The best communicators in your industry or niche are undoubtedly good at shaping people's emotional responses—from telling stories, to remembering people's names, to using humor. They engage people emotionally and shape their responses.

The best teachers are usually good comedians. The best baristas at Starbucks know your name and make you feel included in the community. The best pastors are amazing at telling jokes, parables, and related stories. The best professors raise your level of curiosity to encourage your exploration of the topic. It doesn't matter what industry you are in. You can see these examples every day, in every industry. Shaping people's emotional responses is part of influencing them.

Your fears about overdoing it are well founded, but you need to develop a comfort level with this idea and figure out how to warm up your work with the power of appropriately used emotional triggers. Let's look at some of the common negative responses to using emotion in selling.

"It Is Manipulative to Play with People's Emotions"

The truth is, we are taught from an early age to influence people by ensuring they are in a good mood when we want to ask for something. Whether it's waiting until your dad is in a good mood to ask for money or it's bringing your teacher an apple before the big test, we want to use the subtle art of persuasion to ensure that things go our way. But as we learned in kindergarten, it can take forever for some people to get into a good mood on their own, so telling a joke or making them laugh is a way to get them in the right frame of mind before you ask for something. This is no different in the selling context.

"I've Been Burned by This—and Therefore Hate It"

When you've been the victim of any tactic, whether physical, emotional, financial, or psychological, you develop a strong negative opinion and sometimes an aversion to the topic at large. That's perfectly understandable, but that's not a balanced view of things. You don't avoid cars because you were in a wreck, and so you shouldn't avoid using emotion just because someone manipulated yours. If anything, you can use this sensitivity to your advantage and always be sure that you never cross the line.

"No One Loves My Product or Service— It's a Necessary Evil"

If you sell something that no one can get excited about, then it could certainly be the case that social media isn't the right media to use. Maybe direct marketing is better or perhaps a traditional retail strategy. But if you're a service provider, then before you give up so easily, remember that any service can be sold via social media. Because when you sell a service, you are really selling a relationship. People must like you to choose your service. Your ability to cultivate a relationship with a large number of prospective, current, or former clients will directly impact sales.

"I Don't Want to Be Accused of Manipulating People"

If you use the selling triggers in a constructive and upbeat way, there is truly nothing to stress over. If you overdo it or include emotion in a fake way, then you might be accused of being full of too much hype or be seen as a used car salesman. But chances are, you'll figure out the right balance, and the resulting positive sentiment will start to help you sell.

"I Hate Pressure Tactics"

Everyone hates pressure tactics. But deadlines work to create urgency. Legitimate deadlines will infuse your work with an emotional energy, and if communicated nicely, they won't be seen as a pressure tactic. Pressure tactics are the result of misuse of an emotional approach in a selling context that damages a relationship. They are most frequently used because the seller has urgency due to deadlines, goals, quotas, or other similar motivators. There is no reason to ever use an emotional trigger in a way that breaks a relationship either on Instagram or off.

Weaving It All Together

To get an emotional response from your audience that helps create an upbeat buying mood, you want followers who are truly interested in your product or service. Is it better to have 1,000 true raving fans on Instagram than 10,000 marginally interested fans? I think so! So start with the goal of identifying and serving a core audience. Then share content that they will love. Then weave in the other buying triggers as it's appropriate.

THE SNAPSHOT

(1) Learn to identify the common buying triggers and weave them into your work. (2) If you do it well, people will be upbeat and enthusiastic about your efforts. (3) Learn to identify your own emotional resistance to using selling triggers. (4) The easiest way to get an enthusiastic response to your use of emotional buying triggers is to have followers that are raving fans. Take the time to build your followers strategically so it's not an uphill battle.

Instagram for Nonprofits and Service Providers

nstagram can work very well as a social media tool for both service providers and nonprofits. In both these cases, you are selling without the aid of a physical product for the most part. But if your work has a story that can be shared visually, then you can leverage the Instagram platform regardless of whether you are a for-profit or a nonprofit business. In this chapter, we'll dive into the world of nonprofit marketing as well as for-profit service industry marketing.

As a marketer in your industry, you're undoubtedly familiar with presenting your message in various formats. Generally, you are marketing intangible products—items that cannot be seen or photographed, but they exist nonetheless. Your job is to explain what you do in visual terms. Instagram can help you capture the story of how you serve others in a powerful way. Marketing your work on Instagram is really no different from marketing through other visual media formats. Let's look at the specific approaches that can work for a nonprofit first, and then we'll spend time exploring the unique issues associated with service marketing.

Unique Benefits of Being Mobile

Similar to a for-profit company, a nonprofit or service provider can benefit tremendously from having a social media strategy that includes Instagram's uniquely mobile capabilities. Let's look at the ways a non-profit benefits from being on Instagram:

1. A strong presence on a mobile platform means that your charity is well represented in any geographic location. Why is that important? You want your advocates and fund-raisers to have as much information and support in their local setting as they possibly can. Images help tell stories, and Instagram is a great way for volunteers or advocates to quickly pull up images to help support their presentation of your charity.

2. A strong presence on smartphones allows your fund-raisers or advocates to make a very simple call to action. For example, if you're charity: water, your fund-raisers can simply say something like, "text 'water' to [phone number] now." These types of campaigns are easy to set up with the help of groups like MobileCause.

3. A strong presence on a mobile platform means that you are migrating your desktop-based followers into the mobile space. As the societal trend continues toward a mobile user experience, you won't lose ground in terms of followers.

4. A strong presence on a mobile platform allows you a convenient way to update your followers when you're "in the field." Is your social media marketer in Mexico or South Africa? There is no barrier to immediately updating your followers by posting images on Instagram.

Capturing the Nonprofit Mission Visually

The upcoming chapters in this book related to advertising and monetization all clearly relate to the nonprofit marketer and service provider, but there are some unique issues that we should spend time investigating for these particular user groups. Let's look at the steps involved in the nonprofit marketing process and see if they can be incorporated into your Instagram work.

In Chapter 13, we'll look closely at the AIDA model, which has been around for many years. AIDA stands for *attention, interest, decision,* and *action.* Most nonprofit marketing managers will be very familiar with those steps, but they would apply them a bit differently on Instagram. In a nonprofit context, the approach of these marketing managers might be more similar to these basic steps:

1. **Attention.** The most difficult challenge many nonprofits face is finding prospective donors who care about the cause. Some charities have it easier than others. But every nonprofit marketing manager must ask how the basic mission of the organization can be presented in a compelling way. The initial goal in nonprofit marketing is capturing people's attention. A compelling picture has the power to do that in remarkable ways (see Figure 9.1). Adding a quote to a picture compounds the potential impact and shapes the prospect's thinking.

Figure 9.1 Raising awareness about an issue and asking your followers on Instagram to help you is a fantastic use of the site.

2. **Interest or conviction.** Whereas in the classic AIDA model, the second step is "interest," in the nonprofit world, that step takes on a slightly different form. The nonprofit marketer wants to secure a prospect's strong interest in the general cause, but also in the specific charity. Simply stirring up interest or conviction about a

cause doesn't guarantee that your charity is going to benefit. Many times, charities create concern about a topic, but because they don't clearly sell their solution, they end up creating competitors who will start their own type of response. So this second step—to add interest or conviction—is vitally important (see Figure 9.2).

Figure 9.2 Adding information to an image about an issue helps raise the level of conviction or concern.

3. **Desire to make a difference.** When you're marketing a cause and you get people's attention and interest, it's logical that they are going to want to learn as much as they can about the topic. Part of the natural human tendency is to become an advocate for the issues we find important. The smart nonprofit marketer will feed that fire by providing education, insight, and training for the new converts to the cause, helping to shape their enthusiasm into true affinity and loyalty for the specific charity.

The charity is in a tough spot here because, again, sharing messages that imply that the ultimate solution to the problem is very simple will suggest to people that they can and should start their own charitable response. The desire to make a difference needs to lead to action with the charity that originally raised the issue.

4. **Action.** The action step is the reward for all the hard work. You've gotten people's attention and interest. You've given them a good reason to make a difference, and they've decided to take action. Now the question is simple: *What do you want them to do?*

Taking action can frequently mean simply following you on Instagram or liking your content. It can mean advocating for the cause and your charity. It can mean the giving of time, money, or talent. Can you make a compelling "ask" on Instagram? As shown in Figure 9.3, the team at charity: water is weaving direct asks into its Instagram work. Notice the image's clear call to action, "Donate now," as well as its compelling imagery. You might also notice that the image was liked 1,146 times.

Figure 9.3 Make a clear and compelling invitation (an "ask") and explain how donors can help beneficiaries through your program.

5. **Invitation to participate.** Another common type of call to action in the nonprofit sector is an invitation to attend an upcoming event. It might be a fund-raiser, an annual meeting, or a special event to kick off a new campaign. The classic "save-the-date" card as shown in Figure 9.4 is easy to share on Instagram. It serves as an initial heads-up about an upcoming event.

Figure 9.4 Share your save-the-date postcards and related invitations.

6. **Thanking and reporting back.** Charities have a special opportunity to thank and acknowledge their donors' support. You can thank contributors after a gift is given, and then you can send a special "we appreciate you" type of message or an accomplishment-related message. But all these things can also be shared broadly via Instagram, as shown in Figure 9.5. In this case, charity: water congratulates its followers on Instagram by letting them know that together they have reached $1.7 million toward water projects in Rwanda.

So charities have plenty of ways to leverage the power of the Instagram mobile platform. Did the images in this section capture your interest? They are the work of charity: water, one of the most innovative and effective social media marketing charities around. With more than 75,000 Instagram followers at the time of this writing and an incredibly compelling Instagram profile, charity: water is using the platform brilliantly. Log on to http://www.instagram.com/charitywater to see the latest efforts.

Now let's turn our attention to the service industry and see the ways in which service providers can uniquely use Instagram to grow their business.

Figure 9.5 Report back to donors and thank them for helping you reach short-term goals.

Four Steps to Marketing a Service on Instagram

Service providers have a unique story to tell and a distinct way they market themselves. The truth is, service providers must sell their services, but they must also sell themselves. The customer is buying a long-term relationship, and the quality of the long-term relationship directly impacts the overall impression of the service being provided. Let's look at a few ways they can do this creatively. Goals for a service provider include:

1. **Positioning your brand.** Creating a unique reason to work with you and your company is the first and most critical role of marketing a service firm. Rather than describing what's "industry standard," you want to describe what's completely unique, interesting, and different about you.

2. **Sharing your brand's story.** Just as products have a backstory, your work and commitment to your industry can have a powerful backstory. Charities frequently have a powerful backstory, and although more rare in the service provider space, when you take the

time to articulate your backstory, you have the opportunity to bond with people in a distinctive way.

3. **Defining your attributes.** Are there brand attributes and service-level commitments that you can display visually? Maybe it's a commitment to patriotism, a passion for serving your local community, or a desire to use your business to leave a legacy. Whatever you define as your unique attributes, work to weave them into your Instagram imagery.

4. **Explaining your services.** The warmth and sentiment of building relationships only get converted to income when people clearly understand how you can help them solve a problem. By clearly and simply positioning your services or service-related products, you have a chance to convert your new followers and fans into customers.

Up Close with Laura Lawson Art

Laura Lawson is a 25-year-old artist, photographer, and award-winning blogger. She is also the author of *Believing Is Seeing*, published by SlimBooks. Laura studied fine arts at the Laguna College of Art + Design and has been published in international books and articles dealing with art, social media, and faith. Laura is losing her vision due to a rare degenerative eye condition called retinitis pigmentosa. Since her diagnosis in 2010, she has striven to be a beacon of hope to the blind and low-vision community, pursuing art as fiercely as ever and remaining vigilant in her faith in Jesus. With over 145,000 Instagram followers, Laura shares her unique view of the world with a wide audience (see Figure 9.6).

I asked Laura to share about her first experience with Instagram and how she uses it for business (see Figure 9.7). She said:

I first downloaded Instagram while watching the Super Bowl in February 2011—two years ago now! At first, it wasn't anything more than a way to let my friends know what I was doing on the daily . . . you know, the typical "what I'm eating for lunch" shots. Even now, I use Instagram as a photo diary. It's an amazing thing to be able to look back on little memories forever

lauralawson ▾

LL Author of Believing is Seeing, a story of loss, of heartbreak, of hope, and of a new vision. Pick up your copy for only $5 at slimbooks.com!
http://www.slimbooks.com/believingisseeing

| 1,066 photos | 148,282 followers | 428 following |

Following

Figure 9.6 Laura Lawson uses Instagram to promote her book and art, as well as her fiancé's career as an X Games athlete.

encapsulated in this app. I often enjoy scrolling through my entire feed and reminiscing. As an artist and writer, I use Instagram as a sketchbook to hone my creativity. While I'm not a professional photographer by trade, Instagram has fostered my ability to forge compositions and play around with color. I see compositions for both my paintings and my photos everywhere I go. Additionally, it's fun to post pictures of paintings I'm working on and market my book on Instagram. I haven't necessarily used it directly for marketing myself, but indirectly it's actually become quite useful.

Laura's approach to Instagram images is obviously informed by her training as an artist. I asked her if there were specific things she did to boost her Instagram work, and she described the following approach:

Only a few months after I downloaded Instagram, I gotta admit that I was pretty hooked. I researched photo-editing apps that photographers I admired were using—I currently have about 40 on my phone—and after much trial and error, I now have a go-to routine for editing photos before posting them to Instagram. This includes straightening and sometimes using the clone tool in Filterstorm, playing around with ambience, contrast, and center focus in Snapseed, and almost always using Filter 4 in VSCO Cam. All that being said, aside from learning how to get the most out of expensive iPhone editing apps, it really has been spending time with the people of the Instagram community that has inspired my work the most. I have cultivated innumerable friendships with people, many of whom are lifelong friends, especially in Seattle and San Francisco. These creative people push and inspire me every single day, and I'm so grateful to Instagram for fostering these relationships.

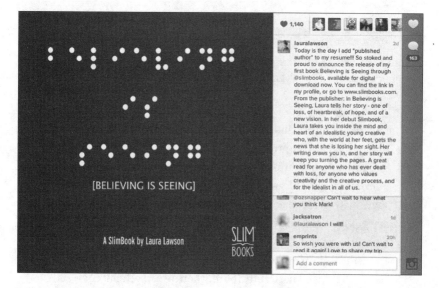

Figure 9.7 The cover of Laura's book, *Believing Is Seeing*, makes an interesting Instagram image.

Laura also uses Instagram to strengthen and grow her business. I asked her to explain how that works, and she said the following:

Because of Instagram, I am able to promote my art, book, and my fiancé's career. I have been invited to take part in mobile photography art shows, social media gigs, several books, and have been interviewed countless times for various media outlets. It has helped to cultivate my name on the web and commanded a certain level of respect in the social media world.

More than anything, I use Instagram for fun. I enjoy talking with brand ambassadors on how to grow their following using the app, but for me, it is first and foremost just a hobby. My success story with Instagram is still evolving. I believe I am just beginning to tap into the benefits of having a large online following. It has led to job opportunities, interviews, writing gigs, and so much more. More than anything, it has led to friendships. I have met truly gifted and creative people all over the country due to Instagram. I believe that nothing is so important in life as relationships.

I asked Laura to share some tips for Instagram users that are new to Instagram. Here is what she had to say to those who are just getting started:

More than anything, I would encourage them to be as interactive as feasibly possible with other users—both people commenting on their photos, and photos they randomly run across that interest them. Follow and interact with others who share common interests or have a similar business. And just have fun with it! A lot of people take Instagram way too seriously. Enjoy it for what it is, and at the end of the day, it's not a popularity contest—just a fun app that is a great way to share your day-to-day life with the world.

I asked Laura to distill her Instagram experience and wisdom down into a few key tips. Here is what she had to share with users:

- Be as interactive as possible.

- Use hashtags, but not excessively, and never use them in your captions.

- Play around with outside photo editing apps. Downloading Snapseed will give you virtually all you need.

- Never post DSLR photos.

- This might be obvious, but the better pictures you post, the more attention you will garner.

- Be creative. It takes time to hone a creative eye, but after a while, you will learn what your followers want to see from you, and you will begin to see square-shaped compositions everywhere.

- Organize a photowalk! Gather other Instagram users together and meet for an hour or two to shoot in your city. Be creative—just about any location can produce cool and unique shots if seen in the right way. I have been a part of photowalks with over one hundred people, and some with just a handful. Both are fun and yield completely different results. You will learn a lot from other people and form some great friendships in the process!

- Don't become obsessed. If you're spending hours each day on your phone, turn it off and go outside. If Instagram becomes more about the documentation of your life than living your life, you've missed the point.

The World Needs Your Service

Your work matters, and by serving others you're making a huge difference in your community and beyond. Who could have imagined a few years ago that your smartphone would provide all the tools you need to share your story and vision with a massive audience?

THE SNAPSHOT

(1) Instagram can work really well for both nonprofit and for-profit service industry marketing. (2) Consider ways to use Instagram in each phase of your marketing work, from asking, to thanking, to reporting back on progress. (3) As a service provider, you are selling a relationship—be sure to consider how Instagram can help position you as a good relational partner. (4) Take Laura Lawson's advice and don't forget to use Instagram for fun.

Branding on Instagram

ou can build your brand's reputation and prestige through Instagram. But it won't happen on its own. Your brand can be substantially helped with the power of Instagram if you take the steps to make it a reality. In this chapter, we'll walk through the issues and challenges of effectively managing your brand through this unique social network. We'll start with the behind-the-scenes issues, such as brand attributes, and then discuss the more practical issues like logos, taglines, watermarks, and other visual elements.

Before you can effectively manage your brand on Instagram, you have to effectively manage it off Instagram. Although we can't dive too deeply into the topic of basic brand management in this book, let's review some of the most basic elements to ensure your Instagram efforts are easily implemented.

Invisible Brand Elements

A brand is the sum of the thoughts and emotions that individuals have about a product or company. When well designed and managed, brands have real power to drive sales. When poorly designed or managed, brands can be very destructive to the cause of the marketer. Brands are more than a logo, more than a color palette, more than a font choice, more than a collection of images or attributes. Brands reside in the mind of the consumer, and until the brand is installed in someone's memory, it doesn't exist for that person.

It becomes a brand when meaning is assigned. The technical word is *semiosis*, or the assignment of meaning to symbols. Semiotics is the study of symbols and their meanings. Your role in defining the brand and installing meaning is the process of identifying your brand attributes and working to convey them in your visual and copywriting work. How do you work to assign meaning? There is a collection of behind-the-scenes concepts you can consider, including:

- **Attributes.** Clarify the attributes you want your brand to have and consistently reinforce them with your copywriting and your product photography. Unfortunately, your attributes cannot simply be what you want the product or corporate brand to stand for; you have to ask these three questions:

  1. What is unique about my product, service, or business?

  2. What do my customers want?

  3. What are my competitors doing?

Your attributes need to land in a unique position within these three questions. A strongly positioned brand features the unique qualities of your product or company, is highly desired by customers, and is different from any of the competition.

- **Personality.** Your brand can have a personality or persona. Think about the differences in personality between Coca-Cola and Red Bull. Both companies are sellers of caffeinated drinks, but they have very different personalities. Red Bull has taken on the adventurer–extreme-doer persona, while Coca-Cola has taken on the role of the innocent and nostalgia-driven classic. How does that play out in real life? Recently, Red Bull sponsored a world-record low-orbit space jump; meanwhile, Coca-Cola launched a commercial featuring an imaginary Santa Claus's workshop inside a snow globe.

  The persona you choose can be expressed in your writing, photography choices, product decisions, and other activities. It is hard work to define a persona and even harder to stick to it over time, but if you do, your subtle message will begin to install itself in the minds of consumers. They will come to know you in that way.

- **Singular idea.** Your brand can have a collection of attributes and a dynamic personality, but it needs to have a singular idea that defines it. You can call it the brand's essence or reason for being. It is the heart of the product, service, or company. Can you think of the singular idea for Apple? BMW? Disney? This singular idea should be the North Star that guides your day-to-day behaviors and helps continuously define your relationship with the customer.

- **Brand story.** You have the opportunity to create a compelling backstory in support of your brand. This can work effectively regardless of whether it is a corporate brand or a product. Think hard about how your brand came into existence and how that story might inspire, encourage, motivate, or entertain others.

- **Positive and negative perceptions.** When customers think about your brand, they will have one of four responses:

  1. No knowledge of your company or product and therefore no emotional response. They are an open book and ready to be influenced by your well-designed brand strategy.

  2. Positive perceptions. This can range from a generally positive perception all the way up to a cultlike enthusiasm.

  3. Negative perceptions. Similar to the wide range of positive responses, there is an equally wide range of negative responses ranging from mild dislike to intense hatred.

  4. Mixed perceptions. Sometimes people really like one aspect of the business or product but dislike another element. In this case they'll provide a mixed review.

Most marketing campaigns are intended to change customer perception, but it's a hard task. When you don't address the underlying issues that customers have a concern over, you'll find it almost impossible to change their point of view.

Visible Brand Elements

When most people think of branding, they think of the visible aspects. These include:

- **Name.** The name is one of the single most important aspects of the brand. A good name can help a business or product be memorable, interesting, and fun to say. A bad name can make it impossible to even pronounce the business or product, much less say anything nice about it.

- **Logo.** Your logo is the visible symbol of your company. There are three basic options: text, a symbol, or a combination of the two.

- **Tagline.** Taglines give you the opportunity to install a little statement or jingle into your prospect's mind—"Red Bull Gives You Wings," "Just Do It," "Like a Good Neighbor, State Farm Is There." A tagline can add real power to your message.

- **Color palette.** Your brand can benefit from a consistent and well-put-together color palette. The opportunity to have a color associated with your brand adds a visual element that helps distinguish you from your competition.

- **Typeface.** Your font choice says something about your brand. It can indicate that you are a fun and informal company or that you are a formal and conservative establishment. Do your best to establish harmony among your typeface, brand persona, and the other visible elements of your brand.

- **Graphics style.** Your customers and prospects can interpret a lot about you by your use of graphics. Are you a young, hip company or a savvy, intellectual firm? Your graphics might answer that question.

The First-Impression Test

Each of the visible and invisible elements adds strength to your brand. You could go to market without all of them put together, but the more these elements are well refined, the stronger your brand is going to be. When prospective customers stumble across your business or product, you want to make as strong an impression as you can. You want them to immediately see you as interesting, polished, easy to understand, and professional. Think back to a time when you stumbled across a new brand that really impressed you. Think about the attributes and elements that got you excited. Chances are, they were well put together.

Leveraging Instagram to Strengthen Your Brand

Instagram is ideally suited to help strengthen and clarify your brand. Here are four ways to accomplish that task:

1. Identify the attributes of your brand and work to use images to represent them. Is "Made in America" an important attribute of your brand? Then you can use patriotic imagery and Americana-themed images to underscore that idea. Try to develop a visual approach to each of your brand attributes.

2. You don't always have to strongly brand each image. You can hint at your brand and leave a bit unbranded on purpose occasionally. Customers are always more excited to discover a product or brand themselves than they are to be beat over the head with it.

3. Work to identify visual metaphors that you can use within your business. A visual metaphor is an image that stands symbolically for something. It's not a concept; it's a symbol that is understood by your fans and followers. Adding deep meaning of this type can be difficult, but when done well, you'll generate very strong responses. A good example is the Product Red campaign (see Figure 10.1). The Product Red concept is a transcendent idea that provides an overarching concept layered on top of otherwise normal products. The transcendent idea? That donating money to HIV/AIDS is a noble idea.

Figure 10.1 The Product Red campaign applies a transcendent concept to otherwise ordinary products and brands.

POWER TIP

A brand's power comes from a combination of the invisible aspects, the visible aspects, and the prospect's experiences with the brand. You have an opportunity to influence all three things.

Visual Brand Strategies in Instagram

The most basic question you'll need to answer is whether you're going to work to add your logo to each image you place on Instagram. There are several options, including the following:

1. Take your image and then work in Photoshop or another image editing tool to add your logo before uploading it back into Instagram.

2. Take your photo in such a way that your logo is included in the picture itself.

3. Use a simple caption app like InstaCap to add your brand or product name. This will unfortunately not likely be consistent with your typeface choices, but at least it is quick and easy.

4. Add a watermark over your photos so they cannot be easily used for commercial purposes. Personally, I dislike this option a lot. In fact, I rarely like images that have a logo, brand, or watermark added.

5. Leave the majority of your images unbranded, but when you share an image of a product, add your brand name or product name.

Indirect Brand Strategies in Instagram

As we discussed, there are invisible attributes of your brand, and you can work to strengthen these on Instagram. For example, you can:

1. Demonstrate your expertise in your niche or industry. You can do that in the caption and comments, not just through the images.

2. Show off your sense of humor. If one of your brand attributes is humor, then you can find unique and creative ways to demonstrate that aspect of your company or product.

3. Reveal your passion for good design. Are you a lover or curator of awesome design? You can show that by sharing and liking exceptional items.

4. Position yourself as socially responsible. Are you trying to demonstrate your support for a cause? You can use Instagram to align yourself with socially responsible activities and products.

Up Close with Dakota Mechanic Studios

Dakota Mechanic Studios is the artist workshop of Brian Lites in Fort Pierce, Florida. Brian is passionate about World War II–era airplanes, and in his workshop he makes functional art out of vintage plane parts. His goal is to stop these classic pieces of World War II–era Americana from being melted down for scrap. He makes clocks, bookends, and other items such as desktop art pieces. He even makes large custom art pieces for special clients. As you might guess, Brian's potential customers are airplane buffs. He gets inquiries from all over the United States as well as Europe. In addition to selling directly to interested customers, he sells items at auction on eBay.

Here is how Brian describes his introduction to Instagram:

> I only discovered IG while searching the App Store on my iPod. The concept intrigued me. I have no formal training as a photographer, but I do enjoy photography. The idea of sharing photos seemed much less involved than keeping up with your status and comments on Facebook. From the first photos that I posted, I began to receive "likes" and comments from interested viewers. Within a short time, I was hooked.

When asked how Instagram supports his business and why he thinks it's a good fit as a marketing tool, Brian said:

> My business deals in making functional pieces and art out of old WWII–era airplane parts. The majority of the photos that I was adding to IG were aircraft photos [see Figure 10.2]. I began to notice that many individuals responding to my posts were pilots, aviation enthusiasts, military personnel, veterans, and airline industry employees. That is when the light came on to the potential IG has in marketing my business. With IG, you have a platform that is free and easy to use, where you can present your product to hundreds or even thousands of people, and spend very little time doing it.

I asked Brian what specific steps he's taken to boost his Instagram work, and he shared these insights:

> I noticed that there were IG users that had large numbers of followers. My first thought was to emulate their approach. But on second thought, I concluded that the quality of my followers, those with the greatest potential of becoming customers, outweighed the quantity of followers. That was my main focus followers is bad. If you focus on your core customers, I believe

Figure 10.2 Brian Lites uses Instagram to identify and cultivate prospective customers for his airplane-related art.

the quantity of followers will come as time goes on. Since my business deals with those in the aviation world, I would much rather have a hundred followers who love airplanes than a thousand followers whose posts consist exclusively of self-portraits in the mirror and photos of One Direction band members. You know what I am talking about. My product line appeals to a smaller customer base than most businesses. I have to be deliberate in gaining followers.

In the Explore tab, I search hashtags that pertain to my potential customers. Since I am dealing with WWII aircraft parts, I search hashtags such as #aircraft, #warbird, #aviation, #airplane, and so on. In viewing a person's photos, I can ascertain whether they have an aviation interest or just happened to take a photo of one airplane. Those who have numerous photos of airplanes are those I follow. Some of the photos are genuinely good photos and deserve comments. By making comments, attention is drawn to my profile page. When people start following my IG page, I view their "followers" and "following" lists. Quite often, there are others in those lists with similar interests. I peruse their photos, make comments, and follow their profile. More often than not, the "follow" is reciprocated. There you have it, one more potential customer.

I asked Brian what advice he might share with a marketer or small business owner that is just getting started with Instagram. Here is his advice:

> I think there is a tendency by some to rush into putting their best photos on IG right away. When you post a photo and hashtag it, the photo is at the top of the hashtag list for a short period of time. It can be very short depending on the hashtags you choose. Spread the posts out. Allow people to see the quality of your work over time. Dumping all your photos in at once leaves nothing good for the future. Only post 1 or 2 photos a day. IG allows you to attach 30 hashtags per post. Use them to gain followers. Your hashtags should pertain to your photo, but can extend beyond that. A Google search will show popular tags such as #instagood, #instamood, #picoftheday, and so on. Interact with fellow IG users. Comment on their photos, like their photos, and follow them. Don't be passive, but rather be proactive in building a base of followers who are prospective customers.

A New Positioning Goal

You have an opportunity on Instagram to position yourself as a visual leader in your industry or niche. You can get a massive head start on the competition by leveraging your brand attributes with this exciting new social media tool. Work to align your visible and invisible brand elements in a way that strengthens and supports your mission; then bring that work into Instagram. If done well, those efforts will lead to profit. In Part 4, we'll talk more about how to use Instagram to sell more products and grow your business.

THE SNAPSHOT

(1) Instagram is an ideal tool for brand building. (2) It's the emotion that resides in the prospect's mind that determines the power of the brand. (3) You can shape those perceptions by managing both the invisible and the visible elements of a brand. (4) Make it your goal to position yourself as a visual leader in your niche or industry.

Part 4

SELLING ON INSTAGRAM

Display Ads on Instagram

ow that we have the basic functions and concepts documented, we can turn our attention to monetization strategies. The first one we'll look into is using Instagram for effective display advertising. In the upcoming chapters, we'll dig into other equally valuable monetization strategies. When you add them all together, you start to realize that you can have a very powerful marketing campaign strategy on Instagram. Let's look at display advertising together.

> **MONETIZATION STRATEGY #1**
>
> Use Instagram like a display ad system to share product information in a compelling way. This old-school advertising approach works perfectly on Instagram. The trick is to combine effective copywriting and images to convey a powerful call to action.

When you weave product photography and copywriting together, you have a classic form of advertising known as display advertising. This type of marketing works well and has been perfected over the last century. Pioneers in direct response marketing created the Sears Wish Book and other early forms of direct mail catalogs. The Sears catalog was a massive advertising book that included product images and copywriting for an incredible number of products (see Figure 11.1).

Figure 11.1 Display ads are a classic form of direct marketing. The *Sears Roebuck & Co. Catalogue* from 1902 provides a lot of fun examples like Dr. Rose's Obesity Powder.

The basic concepts associated with display ads haven't changed very much in over a hundred years. Some of the earliest examples are from catalogs; then the practice expanded to billboards, magazines, and newspapers and eventually moved online. There are even display ads in virtual worlds such as Second Life.

This form of advertising works on Instagram really well. It seems that some things never go out of style. In his incredible book on advertising, *Hey Whipple, Squeeze This,* Luke Sullivan notes that "the crafts of copywriting and art direction, [are] two disciplines that are infinitely portable. Everything you learn about writing and art direction here applies to pretty much every surface you're working on, from bus sides to computer screens" (p. 36).

So when your CEO asks if you have a comprehensive marketing campaign figured out for mobile phones, you get to say, "Yes, we use Instagram as the anchor for our work, and we have adapted our best display ads to that format—we're seeing very encouraging results."

So how do you adapt your best display ads for Instagram? Or how do you create them effectively if you aren't familiar with this process? Let's explore those questions together in this chapter.

It's Cool If It's Cool

There is an unspoken rule in display ad marketing that I'm about to share. Here it is: you can get away with being very direct as long as your target market thinks it's cool. But if the prospects in your target market feel like they're being sold something in an uncool way, prepare to be ignored, unfriended, or even publicly called out.

What's cool for your target market? It will look very different from industry to industry (see Figure 11.2). It will be different for male versus female demographics. And probably the biggest stylistic differences will have to do with the age of your target market.

Figure 11.2 Display ads on Instagram should be a regular part of a marketer's strategy. Alphabet Bags shows us a good example.

Display Ad Techniques

Display ad methods vary over time, and styles are influenced by many factors, including:

- Culture

- Photography techniques

- Language and grammar

- Technology

But there are commonsense guidelines and basic principles that you can start using today. You don't need to be a professional marketer to use these techniques. Let's look at the basic display ad techniques.

Concept #1. People Like Their Likeness

One thing that is common sense to most marketers is that people like seeing images of people in their demographic. They like their own likeness, and seeing ads that have people they can relate to helps them receive the message. Ads working to cultivate 18- to 24-year-olds need to use product photography that shows 18- to 24-year-olds. So the Hollister ads show 18-year-olds without their shirts on. And the Mop & Glo ads show 35-year-old women happily mopping. Again, you probably already knew this; most people do. The only question is, *Can you weave age-appropriate likeness into your Instagram work?*

Concept #2. Humor Works Better Than Fact

If you have the opportunity to weave humor into your ad, you'll do yourself a huge favor. Humor lightens the mood, disarms the antagonistic, and sets the stage for a positive interaction (see Figure 11.3).

Concept #3. Curiosity

The best display ads pique the interest of people so much that they take the initiative to track down further information. Traditional outdoor display ads or print ads had a huge barrier between interest and action. Prospects would have to find a phone and call a number or send away for more information, or in more recent times, they could visit a website or send an e-mail. Old-school marketers learned that developing a very strong sense of curiosity was important, and they found that

Figure 11.3 Humor is a key emotional trigger—using it helps the medicine go down.

including strong calls to action that centered on some type of urgency was best. Limited-time offers, fast-action bonuses, and similar devices are all used to overcome the "I'll do it later" mentality.

To some extent, this same barrier exists on Instagram, but at least the interested consumers are just one click away from getting a link to your website. They simply click on your user profile and click through to the link for your website. Many Instagram advertisers are learning that the old-school techniques still work. The curiosity must be intense, and the call to action clear and urgent.

Concept #4. Showing Is Better Than Telling

Can you use the image in your ad to make a point rather than stating it in the copy? Showing is better than telling, and if you can use photography creatively, your ad will be well received.

At the same time, the image should complement the message, not simply repeat it. There are two tracks to run on when you're creating a display ad, and you should work to optimize both. First, there is the visual concept that includes the image and any on-image copywriting, and then there is the written concept both on the image and off the image. You want to make sure you use both tracks creatively.

Concept #5. Never Be Boring

There are a million and one ways to be boring. Overcoming that common pitfall is hard work. How do you do it? First, you have to work to transcend mediocrity in the image selection process. Second, you have to come up with an approach to the writing that is crisp and authentic. Finally, you have to break through the noise and clutter of Instagram to get noticed.

Concept #6. Get Interesting Visuals from Your Product Photography

Your product has a typical way of being photographed that your customers and prospects are probably very used to seeing. Then there are more artistic approaches. Try your best to get interesting and unique product photography. An interesting image holds people's attention. Add that to an interesting message about the image, and you have the opportunity to engage with prospects in a powerful way.

Concept #7. Avoid Clichés

Every niche or industry has common photos, graphics, and image concepts that are overused. Worse, there are tired words, phrases, and statements that have lost their impact and snap. When you combine predictable imagery with cliché wording, you get a super-boring ad that not only will fail to capture anyone's attention but will also position you as irrelevant, outdated, and uninspired. You don't want to be that marketer; you don't want to be that company.

You'll notice that in the Instagram post by *La Petite* magazine in Figure 11.4, the company uses its magazine cover art as, well, art. The type of photography for a children's magazine is original and so "Renaissance-esque" that it makes a strong statement about the image quality of *La Petite*. The magazine name is the only text, leaving you with one question—what is in this magazine?

Concept #8. Simplify

The most powerful ads focus on one messaging goal, and they crush it. Their simplicity is their strength. Rather than trying to accomplish a

Figure 11.4 *La Petite* magazine uses its cover art as art and makes a huge impact on Instagram.

handful of objectives, you'll need to sacrifice, reduce, boil down, and chop. You'll need to make your image and copy so simple that the concept is fully communicated at first glance.

Concept #9. Start with Your Image

Find a great image and build a story around it. Sometimes an image calls for a certain type of commentary. There is no better way to build an ad than to get a powerful picture of your product, company, or concept and then create an ad concept that expands on the idea that is already inherent in the image.

Prompting Action

Display ads won't convert prospects into enthusiastic buyers unless you use effective strategies to prompt action. Let's look at the specific attributes of highly effective display ads and break down the strategies commonly used:

1. Explain the *unique selling proposition* of the product in a simple way. The core attribute about the product needs to be expressed

candidly and simply. If you're not clear about the unique selling proposition, then the ad readers won't be either. Make it crystal clear so they know whether they need your product or service to solve a problem or not. As the common saying goes, "A confused mind always says no."

2. Give the product a starring role in the ad. Notice in our example in Figure 11.3 that the glove has a prominent role in the ad, almost as if it's a character. In fact, the entire ad is conceived to feature the glove. The clever use of the phrase "5 Finger Discount" ties the image of the glove together with the unique phrase flawlessly. Giving the product a starring role allows the prospect to mentally and emotionally engage with the idea of using the product.

3. Use urgency to close the deal. Like Alphabet Bags did in Figure 11.2, featuring a coupon offer or special deal in your ad can substantially boost response. People procrastinate and delay when it comes to parting with money. Your deadline will help them decide if they really want your product or not. We'll discuss coupon and promotional offers in greater detail in the next chapter.

4. Self-interest is the single most important factor in prompting people to act. Is it in their best interests (not yours) for them to act right now? Getting people to act can be accomplished most directly in how you position the offer. You can position it around you or your company, as in "Year-End Liquidation Sale." Or you can center it on them and their unique situation, as in "Bring in your old TV and get a $50 credit, this weekend only." Focus on them.

5. State the benefits of the product or service, not just the features. You also need to state the benefits of acting now. People don't care as much about the technical features of a product or service as they do the direct benefits they'll receive from getting it.

6. Display ads are experiments. Pay attention to your approach over time and see how tweaking your images and copywriting produces different outcomes. You'll learn what works for your tribe and what doesn't.

One Ad, Many Distribution Channels

Social media platforms are expanding quickly. Many marketers are now engaged on Facebook, Twitter, YouTube, Pinterest, Instagram, and LinkedIn. While this can be a frustration, it also provides an opportunity. Now a small business marketer can effectively do what only large advertising agencies used to be able to accomplish, creating ad campaigns that transcend one social media platform and get seen broadly. How would you do it? Here are a few example steps:

1. Decide on your ad image and message. Make a large-format version and a small-format version, say 600 pixels by 400 pixels for the large format and 300 pixels by 200 pixels for the small format.

2. To launch your campaign, share the large format on Facebook, Pinterest, and Instagram as a photo.

3. Write a blog post about the promotion and embed the smaller image into it.

4. Share the article on Facebook, Twitter, and LinkedIn.

5. Send out a newsletter with the smaller image and tell your newsletter subscribers what you're doing. Ask them to help you spread the word by liking, commenting, sharing, repinning, or retweeting your ad.

6. As people socially share your ad, be sure to thank them by leaving a comment or liking what they've done.

POWER TIP

If you're not a graphic artist, don't worry. There are simple tools that can help you create display ads. InstaCap is an app that lets you add text to images; look for it in the App Store for Apple iOS devices or in Google Play for Android devices.

Up Close with Alphabet Bags

Alphabet Bags, featured in Figure 11.5, is an accessories brand creating lovely items with an emphasis on the simple, bold, and cheerful. Let's look more closely at how the company uses Instagram for effective marketing. If you want to check the company online, you can visit @alphabetbags or http://www.instagram.com/alphabetbags.

Figure 11.5 The Alphabet Bags Instagram page, http//www.instagram.com/alphabetbags

Alphabet Bags was born in a spare room in the East Dulwich area of London in 2008 as a result of a shared love of typography, the alphabet, and simple totes. Cofounders Lucas and Hayley are a husband-and-wife team in their twenties. They explained:

> Alphabet Bags launched quite simply with 26 cotton totes printed with every lovely letter from A to Z. People sure seemed to like them, and this not only made us very happy, but it also encouraged us to carry on designing new things. We now have a whole bunch of collections including initial coin purses, colorful totes for summer, wash bags, a wedding collection, and more typographic totes than you can shake a stick at. We are always working on new things, and boy do we have big plans!

The couple launched their Instagram work in August 2011, and they remember how Instagram began to work for them:

As we began to network with other small businesses via Instagram and started to hear from customers that they had discovered our site through Instagram, we realized that it could be a really valuable tool for our brand. It was really nice for us to see our customers taking pictures of our products and packaging and sharing these with their followers and us too. Many of our Instagram followers have found us through other Instagram users who have posted photos of their orders.

When it comes to efforts to boost their Instagram marketing efforts, they note:

We try to post pictures every day now, but are careful not to post too many or anything that's not going to be of interest to our followers. We feel it's useful for our brand to post new products, snapshots of our office, and behind-the-scenes photos, as well as more personal photos (as we're a small family business). It's nice to give our customers a glimpse into our personal lives and interests as well as our work and products.

When asked what Instagram has done for their business, they said:

Instagram has certainly had a positive effect on our business. It has been an excellent way to get our brand out there and a really nice way to connect with customers and keep them informed. Previously, most of our contact with customers was done via an e-mail newsletter; now Instagram is an equally important way for us to keep in touch with fans of Alphabet Bags. Instagram is much more instant than a newsletter though, and much more fun to use! It has become a daily part of our lives, and we really enjoy posting photos as well as browsing other users' photos.

Alphabet Bags recommends the following best practices for new Instagram marketers:

1. Don't post too much, especially in quick succession, and take time to create interesting setups.

2. Boring photos are boring; make sure the images you post are nice and/or interesting.

3. Think about angles and lighting when taking your pictures. If you make sure there is good lighting in your photos, the Instagram filters will look their best, or you won't need to use a filter at all.

4. Find and follow users who interest you; it's a great way to connect with like-minded people.

5. Try to follow as many like-minded people or businesses as you can find. It's a great way to connect with other brands and interesting individuals, and often they follow you back, so it's a great way to build up your followers too.

6. If you have cats or dogs, make sure you post plenty of photos of them!

THE SNAPSHOT

(1) Instagram is ideal for display ad marketing. (2) Start with a powerful image and define the message to complement it. (3) The message must be simple and direct. (4) Use your effective display ads across all your social media platforms like a classic ad campaign.

Using the Power of Free

There is no greater selling device than giving away something for free as a way to prompt engagement. It works across industries and in all sorts of situations. From free samples at Costco to free Kindle e-books on Amazon, people love free things. If you want to sell a lot of products or services, learn to leverage the power of free.

In his groundbreaking book *Free: The Future of a Radical Price* (2009), Chris Anderson explains how innovative companies are using free as a competitive tool:

> Companies look at a portfolio of products and price some at zero (or close to it) to make other products, on which they make healthy profits, more attractive. Technology is giving companies greater flexibility in how broadly they define their markets, allowing more freedom to give away some products to promote others.

In this chapter, we'll look specifically at four very different monetization strategies that all leverage the power of free. First we'll talk about the concept, and then we'll apply it to Instagram and discover how Instagram can help support each of them. Finally, we'll get up close with the owner of *La Petite* magazine and see how she is using Instagram to grow the business.

If you have products, you have an opportunity to use the power of free; and if you're a service provider with no product to offer, keep reading—this chapter is for you, too. The power of free can be leveraged for service businesses just as easily as for product-focused businesses.

Before we dive into the monetization strategies, let's look at the differences between using the power of free and simply slashing your prices. You'll see that I am not a big fan of discounting your prices through short-term sales, such as the classic "25% off today only" or similar coupon strategies. As an entrepreneur trying to focus on profit margins, I strongly dislike those gimmicks either off Instagram or on it. Those don't help you grow your business; they help you destroy your profits, so I won't be recommending them. Let's look at the reasons why.

Free Versus Discounting

Using free items strategically is very different from discounting your prices. Using free items is a strategy that can work very effectively, but discounting generally does real damage. If you're in the habit of running sales constantly to try to generate business, then consider this chapter an alternative plan that is healthier than your current practice.

Let's explore the problems with frequently running sales or issuing discount coupons. When you run sales and simply discount your prices, you are doing the following:

1. You are putting your customers in a chronic state of waiting for the "next big sale." While issuing a 20 percent–off coupon or running a storewide sale boosts response in the short term, in the long term it has the opposite effect. Your customers come to expect you to periodically mark down your items. Frugal customers will wait you out, and many purchases that could have been achieved at full price are conducted at a less profitable price. You don't want to create a waiting game with your customers—you'll lose.

2. The message you are sending when you put your work on sale is that the "true worth" is less than the originally stated price. That's not a message you want to send. It cheapens your product or service.

3. Coupons and discounts work like a drug in your sales system. Yes, you can become addicted to coupons. How does it work? Coupons

give you an unrealistic boost of everything: customer traffic, enthusiasm, and sales. But the effect wears off quickly, and you want to do it again. The next time you need quick cash, you'll think of one thing—coupons. Your addiction will grow, and it will kill your business.

4. By selling a large portion of your inventory or service at a lower-than-desired price, you erode profit margins. Over the long term, the only thing that creates wealth is your profit margin. If your company lives on a 20 percent profit margin and you begin discounting your prices, that number will quickly shrink. Ideally, you'll find ways to grow your profit margin, not shrink it. Coupons and discounts shrink it.

5. Coupons suppress creativity. Coupons and sales are easy, and when you do them, you don't work to find the harder, more interesting customer engagement activities that can produce similar results. There are things you can do to boost traffic, enthusiasm, and sales without destroying your profit margin, but they take some creative thinking.

Strategies for Using Free Items

Of course, these strategies aren't necessarily unique to Instagram, but they work well on it. Ultimately you have to settle on a creative use of free and then ask yourself which social media platform will do the best job in support of the effort. Maybe it's Facebook, maybe Pinterest, maybe Instagram, or maybe all of them at the same time for one big social media campaign. Frequently, smart marketers are finding that Instagram does a nice job. Let's look at four strategies together and how to use Instagram to fully leverage them.

Giveaways

Giving away one of your products, or a service, is a great way to get attention. There are countless variations on this theme, and you'll have to decide how it works best for your business, but it does work to energize prospective as well as existing customers.

> **MONETIZATION STRATEGY #2**
> Instead of constantly issuing coupons, switch to exciting giveaways. The overall cost of your efforts will decrease substantially, and if done well, you'll generate the same level of buzz and enthusiasm.

In some business contexts, the product or service can be given away once or twice a year as part of a big campaign. In other business contexts, it makes sense to have a product or service that is always free. We will explain this model more thoroughly later in the chapter.

Why is giving away a product or service better than a coupon or sale? There are lots of reasons, including:

1. When you give away a product, you don't cheapen its perceived value.

2. People assume that you are doing the giveaway as a promotion, but they do not assume any other negative ideas—for example, that you have too much excess inventory and need to lower the price to get people to buy it.

3. The attention from and impact on prospective customers can be very high, even higher than with a 10 percent–off coupon. This is achieved without actually giving them anything of value other than hope.

4. The ultimate cost of the promotional effort using a free item is much cheaper than giving everyone a 10 percent discount.

5. Part of the risk involved in a coupon giveaway, or running a sale involving a certain percentage off for a certain amount of time, is that you don't know how many people will take you up on your offer, and therefore you don't know the total cost of the campaign to your bottom line. When you use a giveaway, you know exactly how much it will cost you before you start.

6. If done correctly, you can collect e-mail addresses from the interested prospects and introduce them to your business through an ongoing e-mail campaign.

One giveaway strategy that we have used effectively at Liberty Jane Clothing is our "12 Days of Christmas" campaign. The reason we run it is fairly simple. Customers are so accustomed to holiday sales, particularly on Black Friday, that you run the risk of looking asleep at the wheel if you don't do one. But we don't like the idea of doing a Black Friday sale for the reasons mentioned above, so instead we run a fun giveaway. Here's how it works.

Each day for 12 days we do a giveaway. The items being given away are a surprise until that day. They are announced and shared on our blog, Facebook, and Instagram. The giveaway on day one is a single item, on day two it's two items, and so on. The items are various products that we think our customers might enjoy. By the twelfth day, the energy and excitement are intense. One year, as you can see in Figure 12.1, we gave away 11 pairs of shoes on the eleventh day. To enter to win, you simply leave a comment on our blog answering a specific question. The winner is chosen at random.

Figure 12.1 The Liberty Jane Clothing "12 Days of Christmas" giveaway is an example of the power of free.

The questions are scripted in a way that either gives us good customer feedback or helps us build our brand. One question was, "My experience with Liberty Jane Clothing has been . . ." There were

280 heartwarming responses to that question. The twelfth-day give-away question had 578 responses.

Special Offers or Coupons

Another great promotion using the power of free is to give away a product or related service. The classic buy-one, get-one (BOGO) sale is one form of this strategy. Providing free shipping for a limited time is another form of special offer. The downside of this type of strategy is that, similar to putting your items on sale, you don't know the full cost of the promotional campaign until it is over. This type of strategy is the most similar to putting items on sale via coupon, and your customers can come to see it that way. BOGO is very similar to 50 percent off when you buy two. For that reason, we don't use this type of promotion very often.

> **MONETIZATION STRATEGY #3**
>
> Create a special offer, such as free shipping or BOGO. These types of offers are a step up from offering coupons or putting items on sale.

Contests That Engage

Contests work really well on Instagram, and as of this writing, they are allowed under the TOS. But you should check to confirm that there hasn't been a change in policy before launching a contest. The reason for the caution is because Facebook, the parent company of Instagram, has become very strict about how contests can be conducted. Let's hope Facebook allows Instagram to keep things as is.

> **MONETIZATION STRATEGY #4**
>
> Create a fun contest using Instagram. Effective contests can generate a flood of interest and enthusiasm.

There are many types of contests, and you'll want to consider how best to conduct one to support your brand. The ModCloth "Name It & Win It" contest is a good example of an easy-to-achieve Instagram contest. You can see how the company structured the rules in Figure 12.2. Notice the 2,357 likes and over 3,000 comments.

Figure 12.2 The ModCloth "Name It & Win It" contest is a good example of an easy-to-conduct Instagram contest.

The reason we like this contest model is because the entry method is right on the image. There is no secondary site involved and no hashtag. This maximizes participation and allows people to jump in quickly.

Free Digital Products

When traditional businesses integrate a collection of free digital products into their business model, they can see substantial benefits. In this approach, rather than using free as a short-term gimmick to get interest and attention, the marketer takes free to a much deeper level and allows customers to get something of real value in exchange for something that is nonmonetary, like an e-mail address. Let's look at the benefits of using this type of free product and how Instagram can support it; then we'll wrap up this chapter by looking at several examples.

> **MONETIZATION STRATEGY #5**
>
> Offer a digital product in exchange for the prospect's e-mail address. Advertise the free product on Instagram and explain how the prospect can get it. As part of the free product, explain your story and how your paid products or services are superior. Follow up with related offers and relationship-building messages.

While this method of prospect engagement has been around for many years, people who are referred to as "Internet marketers" pioneered this business model in its digital form. The benefits associated with the practice are clear and easy to evaluate. Let's look at the benefits of introducing a free product line into your existing business:

1. A free product line, if done right, attracts the attention of your ideal customers and gets them into a relationship with you. This is the proverbial foot in the door, which cannot be underestimated in a crowded marketplace.

2. A free product line, when offered properly, acts as an ethical bribe to get the customer to act in beneficial ways. Give away a free e-book on a related topic in order to get the customer's e-mail address. Give a free how-to guide to everyone that likes your Facebook fan page in order to get more Facebook likers.

3. A free product line, if marketed aggressively, allows you to disrupt your marketplace and turn your competitors' products into nonmonetary tools. Does your competitor sell a fancy how-to guide? Give yours away for free in exchange for the customer's e-mail address; then upsell the customer on a more complete guide that is not free. Does your competitor depend on revenue from a traditional book? Give away a similar e-book for free and upsell readers on a "not-free" printed version to win market share.

The James Bond Approach

James Bond and his helpful tech guru Q have a tried-and-true method for being awesome. They slide their lifesaving technology into innocent-looking items that slip by unnoticed past people's defenses. The laser goes into the ballpoint pen. The parachute goes into the tuxedo jacket. The truth serum goes into the quarter pounder with cheese.

Famous copywriter Bob Bly calls this "putting the pill in the meat." It means that you include your harder-to-convey information in information that is more easily accepted. Want someone to read a three-page backstory about how your company was founded? Good luck, because on its own, that dog won't hunt. But if you put it into a free report about how customers can cut their expenses in half, not only will it be readily accepted, but prospects will read it with interest. As Mary Poppins said, a spoonful of sugar makes the medicine go down.

When you give something away for free, like a how-to guide, you have the opportunity to include the following types of valuable but hard-to-convey information:

1. Your company's mission, vision, and values.

2. Your founding story.

3. Your product's unique selling proposition and reason for existence.

4. Your philosophical approach to your product or craft.

5. Upselling and cross-selling explanations—how your products all fit together to serve the customer.

6. Your seasonality, annual cycle of production or design, and product design process.

7. Your customer service approach, methods, and practices.

8. Your commitment to your product or service and guarantee of satisfaction or happiness—in other words, a longer explanation of your guarantee.

9. Your future plans and upcoming projects. Sharing what you're going to do next allows prospective customers to buy into your vision and get excited about what you're going to do next.

Using Instagram to Promote Free Products

The display ad–friendly nature of Instagram allows you to effectively share your free content with your followers in an exciting way. Everyone appreciates something for free, and by positioning these products as a gift to your followers, you have an opportunity to build strong customer loyalty. Let's look at ways to use Instagram to help create this positive situation:

1. Share a how-to tip that is fully visible right on Instagram. This is more work than just snapping a picture, but it could be well worth it. To accomplish this, use Photoshop Elements to create a square image with the how-to content on it. Then simply e-mail it to yourself, open the e-mail on your phone, and save the image to your image library. From there, you simply upload it to Instagram like any other image.

2. Create a longer how-to, place it on your website or blog, and then advertise it on Instagram with a nice display ad type of image.

3. Create an e-book and share the cover on Instagram with a description about the e-book in the image's caption.

4. Create a ritual of sharing something free at a set interval. Many bloggers use a "Freebie Friday" methodology that helps prospects and customers come to appreciate visiting their website regularly. This system could work monthly or even annually, such as offering a free e-book each January.

Up Close with *La Petite* Magazine

La Petite magazine started its Instagram marketing in February 2012. As Figure 12.3 shows, the company has over 4,000 followers.

La Petite magazine is an online magazine focused on children's fashion and design. Here is how the owner describes the company's journey onto Instagram:

> My friend told me about Instagram, and I thought it was a great way to connect with other people and spread the word about

lapetitemag ·

La Petite Magazine A magazine full of inspiration for the little ones! Tag your kids pictures with #lapetitemag for a chance to be an upcoming model in one of our issues
http://lapetitemag.com

Follow

| 161 photos | 4,041 followers | 99 following |

Figure 12.3 The team at *La Petite* magazine uses amazing product photography to cultivate a following on Instagram.

my business, *La Petite* magazine. I began to realize that Instagram was a great advertising tool! I got an e-mail from a couple people who started following me on Instagram. They proceeded to tell me in the e-mails that they followed the link from my Instagram to my *La Petite* site, and now are huge fans of my magazine and blog! I knew then that Instagram was valuable for my business! I have had the opportunity to meet so many amazing people that I don't think I would have got to connect with if it wasn't for Instagram! Also, it has increased our revenue. We have gotten more ads because of Instagram. This definitely has changed our business!

The team at *La Petite* suggests the following best practices for new Instagram marketers:

1. Like other users' pictures. Set aside time during the day to do this. Don't just like people you follow; it is more important to like others' photos whom you don't follow!

2. Get personal and comment on others' pictures.

3. Get on Statigram. Statigram is a great online tool for helping you find out your Instagram statistics and when the best time of day is

to post a picture. It also tells you about your follower engagement and the likes you have received, etc. Statigram will also show you the followers you have lost and gained.

4. Start using a hashtag for your business.

5. The biggest mistake is posting too many photos in one day.

6. Integrate with Pinterest. We pin a lot of images from our Instagram to our Pinterest page. We find this helps with followers and likes.

THE SNAPSHOT

(1) You can use the power of free on Instagram to build your brand. (2) Set a date to launch a contest on Instagram and see how it resonates with your target market. (3) Create a helpful free product and begin advertising it on Instagram. (4) Don't forget to put the pill in the meat.

Chapter

13

Multistep Campaigns

*U*sing the power of free isn't the only way to conduct marketing on Instagram. There is another campaign style many marketers are using very effectively. It goes by different names, but I refer to these campaigns as "multistep" campaigns because they involve multiple steps. Each step is designed to do a specific part of the marketing job. When you put them together, you have a strong marketing plan that works very well.

In this chapter, we'll look at the concept of multistep campaigns and how they've evolved. Then we'll examine the two common forms of the approach being used on Instagram. Finally, we'll focus in on how we use this kind of campaign in an ongoing way at Liberty Jane Clothing to sell shoes for two to three times more than the competition.

The Origin of the AIDA Model

A multistep Instagram marketing campaign is a campaign that involves an unveiling of details or messages over an extended period of time. Through several steps, the marketer works to capture attention, pique interest, create a desire to buy, and then call the customer to action. These steps aren't new to most marketers; they are known as the classic AIDA marketing formula (attention, interest, desire, action). It is the basis for most marketing campaigns today.

Although AIDA isn't new, the journey of how it started showing up on Instagram is worth understanding. From the print advertising world of 1899, to the direct response marketers of the 1950s, to the Internet marketers of the 1990s, to the smartphone marketers of today, AIDA has stood the test of time and been adapted to many different forms. Its application to smartphones via Instagram is another step in its evolution. Let's look at how it got there.

Fred Macey's Breakthrough in Advertising

A catalog marketer named Fred Macey first wrote about the four-step plan that has become known as AIDA in 1899. That year, the Bissell Carpet Sweeper Company held a contest and asked Macey to be the expert judge. The contest was to see who could make the best advertisement for Bissell's carpet-cleaning machines. Macey's guidelines were described as follows:

> 1st. The advertisement must receive "Attention," 2d. Having attention it must create "Interest," 3d. Having the reader's interest it must create "Desire to Buy," 4th. Having created the desire to buy it should help "Decision." ("The Bissell Prize Advertisement Contest," *Hardware*, March 1900, p. 44, from Wikipedia)

The AIDA Model Goes Serial

In Minneapolis in 1925, the Burma-Shave company started using roadside signs to sell its product—shaving cream. The signs became a hallmark of outdoor display advertising in the early years of the American highway system. The Burma-Shave signs were developed to contain six brief messages, each message on a different sign. As drivers would pass them, the full message of the campaign would be revealed. The sign campaigns ran successfully from 1925 through 1962. An example of the sign messages is as follows:

Our fortune
Is your

Shaven face
It's our best
Advertising space
Burma-Shave

As roads improved and speeds increased, it became a less effective way to use the AIDA model. But the concept of using AIDA in a multimessage serial way was born. The breakthrough was that you could break the AIDA model into multiple messages and share them over time. Although the roadside signs ended, AIDA moved on to new platforms, including direct mail.

The AIDA Model Goes Postal

Direct response marketers became very accustomed to using the AIDA model. Direct mail, it seemed, was a natural way to apply the method. The best direct response marketers and agencies perfected the model through constant testing and refinement. Over time, they learned that advertisements that were longer, with lots of copy and product information, were better than shorter-form ads. Through the long-form letter, you have the chance to fully develop each of the elements of the AIDA model. The customer gets engaged, convinced, and, through involvement, sold.

The AIDA Model Goes Virtual

By the 1990s the AIDA model was very common in all forms of direct response marketing. It worked in display ads in newspapers and magazines, outdoor display ads, direct mail, and television, and it was about to find its way onto the Internet.

The first version of the AIDA model on the Internet was simply an adaptation of the long-form sales letter, modified for web pages. The beauty of this version of the AIDA model was that a shopping cart link could be included in the ad, allowing good copywriters to immediately make sales. Yet another context, but again, the AIDA model worked.

Soon Internet marketers realized that capturing e-mail addresses and sending prospects a series of messages to generate a sale was yet another version of the model. The system, still very much used today, includes two steps. First, the marketer captures the e-mail address from a prospect in the targeted niche or industry, and then in subsequent e-mail messages the marketer uses the AIDA model to sell all sorts of related products in that niche.

Jeff Walker's Breakthrough Adaptation

Jeff Walker, a Colorado-based Internet marketer, is widely regarded as a pioneer in adapting the AIDA model to the task of launching a product on the Internet in a serial way. Jeff wrote a stock market newsletter and wanted a way to engage prospective customers with the hope of signing them up for his monthly paid subscription. Starting with a very small list, and with the AIDA model in serial form adapted to the Internet, he built a six-figure business in six days. His use of the model worked.

He first used e-mails as the method to share the AIDA content as separate but related messages. Later, he pioneered the use of videos to engage with prospective customers. His approach was to break the long-form sales letter into a series of unique messages, each building toward the launch of the product. He called it the "sideways sales letter." It was the AIDA model in a serial format, a la Burma-Shave signs, applied to an information product launch.

Jeff has helped literally thousands of marketers adapt this model to their products. It works for both physical and digital products and for low-value items as well as very high-priced items. Our first use of his model was in support of our Design Academy program. It is a $79 course that teaches people the basics of effective fashion design. We run it a few times a year. Before using his model, we averaged 20 students per class. When we used his system to market the course, we had over 100 students enroll. We were shocked at the effectiveness.

The AIDA Model on Instagram

As you might guess, the AIDA model has found its way onto Instagram. There are two primary models in use. Let's look at each one and see how it might apply to your business. The first one is rather obvious; the second one might take you more time to learn but might end up having a larger impact on your business.

The Two-Step Lead Generation Model on Instagram

You only focus on one of two goals when you are a direct marketer: to get a lead for a future sale or to get a sale. There is no other outcome you are focused on. The two-step lead generation model is designed to accomplish the first goal—getting a lead. The basic premise of any social media site is, in some ways, a two-step lead generation methodology. The steps involved in a two-step lead generation model are as follows:

1. Capture the prospects' attention and then pique their interest. The call to action is to have them follow you on the site.

2. Effectively market to your followers. If you're on Instagram, Pinterest, Facebook, YouTube, or Twitter, you're using a two-step lead generation model. But you didn't need to buy this book to learn that you're supposed to get people to follow you on Instagram and then market to them.

MONETIZATION STRATEGY #6

A two-step lead generation strategy has the goal of either making a sale or getting a lead. Your work on Instagram is a form of a two-step lead generation system.

The difference between a social media two-step lead generation process and a more traditional two-step process is that in the more traditional setting, you are focused on getting an e-mail address or mailing address. Then the second step is done via those media. You can use Instagram to complete this strategy very simply. Just advertise a free product on Instagram and let people know that to get their free copy they need to visit your website or landing page. On that site, you collect their e-mail address, and then you fulfill the promise of delivering the free product.

The Visual Product Launch

Let's look at the second type of multistep campaign in more detail. You may be less familiar with this type of campaign strategy, so I'll spend more time explaining it. It is working very well for lots of companies on Instagram. Let's jump into this technique, which I call a "visual product launch."

Not only is a visual product launch on Instagram possible, but it is also easy. It is an adaptation of the AIDA model in the tradition of Jeff Walker's product launch method, but it has been applied to Instagram using pictures as the primary marketing content. This model is yet another twist on the AIDA model and is clearly working for the pioneering marketers that are implementing the approach on Instagram. The exciting part about this is that it represents the AIDA model being used on smartphones. The timeless model lives on once again, this time in a postcomputer way.

> **MONETIZATION STRATEGY #7**
>
> A visual product launch allows you to tell the story of a new product visually. You give prospects a peek as the product comes together, and it builds anticipation and enthusiasm.

Each business will implement the visual product launch strategy differently, but in general, the strategy conforms to the following steps. See if you can adapt them to your situation.

1. **Attention.** Share an image of a new product and explain what you're working on. This is a way of revealing a new product in a manner that will get people's attention. Frequently this is a physical product, but it could also work well for a digital product. The picture can be a behind-the-scenes photo, or it might be a picture of the "under-construction" version of the product. It can also be a picture that positions the product in a fun or interesting way. Your goal is to capture people's attention and get them to take notice. Having your followers like or comment on your new image is a bonus action. The main goal is to have them be excited to have seen it.

2. **Interest.** Build interest and enthusiasm by sharing pictures of the behind-the-scenes work involved in launching the product. Answer questions that people ask in the comment section and explain further details. This step is important for two reasons: First, to capture people's interest by sharing the images and information. Second, to gauge people's interest and learn from their input. If you frequently use the visual product launch strategy for products, you'll begin to see differences in the level of enthusiasm and learn more about your customers' preferences and interests.

3. **Desire.** People want what they can't have. It's human nature. So part of the visual product launch strategy is to put out images and information prior to the item being available as a way to intensify people's desire. By announcing a specific product launch date, you escalate people's anticipation for getting the item and give them time to plan for the purchase, building up a level of excitement.

4. **Action.** The beautiful part of the visual product launch strategy is that because you've done a lot of preselling, you can do a very soft close. The prospective buyers will be very enthusiastic to buy. In fact, if you've done the first three steps effectively, the call to action can be very matter-of-fact.

Closing the deal and confirming the order will look different for different products and services, but there are two common elements. First, if the product or service is going to be limited in some way, then the call to action needs to have the clear dates or other details. If the product is going to be a part of your regular ongoing catalog of offers, then it is frequently a good idea to give some type of extra benefit to the people who are your initial buyers. These can look different for different circumstances, but it can frequently take the form of a launch bonus for the first 1,000 buyers, or perhaps it could be an extra gift for people who order during the first day. Give them something tangible, practical, and generous.

Up Close with the Little Janes Product Launch

At Liberty Jane Clothing, we recently launched a new style of doll shoes that we call Janes. They are doll-sized alpargatas shoes, also known as espadrilles, like the very popular TOMS brand. Here is how we used Instagram to conduct a visual product launch. As an important side note, we make these shoes in small batches by hand in the United States, and we always immediately sell out when we make them available for purchase. Here is how we use Instagram to help us achieve this success.

Step #1. Attention

In the attention-getting step, we strive to position an image as fascinating, unique, fun, or compelling. This will be different for each company—and very different from one niche to another. For our Janes, we took this simple image shown in Figure 13.1.

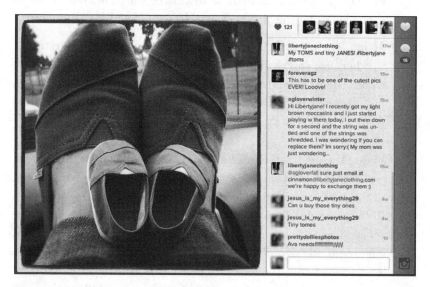

Figure 13.1 To get people's attention, we showed Janes next to TOMS.

Step #2. Interest

In the interest-getting step, we strive to share a message that informs people who are attracted by the original picture. Our interest step, as shown in Figure 13.2, was to show another product image with the following message: "Behind the scenes, getting the JANES ready to list!"

Figure 13.2 This image and message is meant to do one thing—attract prospect's interest.

Step #3. Desire

In the desire stage, our goal is to provide another sneak-peek image and give an update on the status of the product. In the case of our Janes, as Figure 13.3 shows, we shared another image and then added this message: "Red JANES coming soon to Liberty Jane Clothing!"

Figure 13.3 In the desire stage, we provide more exciting pictures and a message to build enthusiasm.

Step #4. Action

In the action step, we simply mentioned to people that the shoes were available and included a smiley face (see Figure 13.4). No pressure, no hard sale, just the facts.

Figure 13.4 In the action stage, we simply let people know the shoes are available. No pressure tactics are necessary.

An Integrated Visual Product Launch

Conducting a visual product launch and only using Instagram as the launch platform is probably a serious mistake. The only reason I can imagine doing it is to test the efficacy of the Instagram platform to drive sales—in other words, as an experiment to examine the power of Instagram. As with any other site, there are pros and cons to using it for any job. Let's look at the pros and cons briefly and then discuss what an integrated campaign might look like.

Pros

- A visual product launch on Instagram is a launch optimized for smartphones. There is a lot of wisdom in that!

- Images are generally the most powerful product-selling devices.

- You can leverage hashtags to expand your reach beyond your usual followers.

Cons

- The Instagram platform only allows for a very short-form copywriting strategy, which is unfortunate.

- Instagram is a feed-based distribution system, so there is a good chance that even your followers won't see your image. They might not be on Instagram when you share it.

- There is no ability to share a direct link to your e-commerce site. You can include the URL, but it won't have an active hyperlink. Maybe this will change in the future, but for now it is a drawback.

Unless you're running an experiment, an ideal product launch will leverage your existing social media and web assets, including, of course, e-mail. Why not bring all your weapons to the battle? Your goal is to use each social platform for its highest and best use: images on Instagram and Pinterest, videos on YouTube, quick updates on Twitter. Facebook can serve as a host for almost any type of content, and so any images you create can be shared on Instagram and Pinterest and then published to Facebook. Videos can be shared on YouTube and then published to Facebook and Pinterest. All your content can potentially be included, or at least mentioned, in e-mails. An ideal visual product launch will include a collection of e-mail messages that use your rich media content and help expand and explain the basic story.

In Part 5, we'll work to integrate Instagram with your other social media platforms. There are specific tactics and actions you can take today to extend and improve the power of your Instagram work. When you combine Instagram in this way, you make each of your social media platforms stronger.

THE SNAPSHOT

(1) You can consider Instagram a two-step lead generation system. (2) The goal of these types of systems is to either make a sale or get a lead. (3) Learn to use the AIDA model on Instagram to instill a sense of enthusiasm for your products. (4) Master the visual product launch strategy on Instagram.

Part 5

INTEGRATING INSTAGRAM INTO YOUR ONLINE MARKETING

Integrating Instagram with Your Website

our ultimate goal for all your social media sites should be to ensure support for your sales goals. The day is coming when you will be able to sell directly on the social media platforms, but until then, traffic needs to be driven to your e-commerce site. That goal applies to Instagram as well. In this chapter, we'll look at all the options available to ensure visitors start on Instagram and end on your website making a purchase.

The Two-Way Street

It might seem counterintuitive, but the traffic should be a two-way street. We need to ensure that visitors start on your website and end up on Instagram as a new follower. Why would you want to drive traffic off your website and out to a social network? There are four important reasons:

1. Getting people to follow you on a social network is another point of connection. You want them connected to your company in as many ways as possible.

2. Having customers follow you on Instagram ensures that you can market to them later. Generally, if you haven't captured their e-mail address or gotten them to follow you on a social media site,

your chances of proactively marketing to them in the future is highly diminished.

3. Instagram is all about mobile marketing. Having people go from your website to Instagram and follow you means that you can market to them in the future via their smartphone. That moves your marketing campaign into the mobile marketing game in a new and exciting way.

4. People might love your website and products, but they cannot share them with their friends in an easy manner until they jump onto a social network. If you drive them to a social network, you run a very good chance of them liking you, following you, commenting, or sharing. You want the word-of-mouth marketing to kick in, and that only happens on the social sites.

Getting People from Your Website to Their Phone

You might be confused about how you can have people look at your website via their computer and then begin following you on an app for their phone without leaving the computer, picking up their phone, and searching for your website or Instagram profile. Obviously that is a confusing set of steps.

Until late 2012, there was no practical way to solve this disconnect directly within the Instagram system. Many marketers would use a third-party site, Statigram, to help solve this dilemma. Statigram serves as a web viewer of your Instagram account, so that computer users can view images and, most importantly, begin following you. This practice is still in use, as many marketers set up their web integration efforts with Instagram and Statigram and have not yet taken advantage of Instagram's new web-based profiles.

In late 2012, Instagram launched its web profiles. This allows computer users to easily view and follow Instagram users. It also allows webmasters and marketers to construct a seamless path from a company website to their Instagram profiles so visitors can easily navigate from the website to the Instagram profile without needing to pick up a smartphone. But the next time they do pick up their smartphone and use Instagram, your images will be visible in their Home tab's feed of photos. Your profile will also show up in the list of profiles they are following.

POWER TIP

On your website, set up the Instagram social sharing buttons to point to the web version of your Instagram profile, such as http://www.instagram.com/libertyjaneclothing. People will use that path to follow you, and the next time they are browsing Instagram on their smartphone, they'll see you as someone they follow.

When they like your images, it will be shared with their friends via the News Feed. These activities serve to integrate you, your brand, and your products into their mobile experience in a long-lasting way.

So the navigation challenge has been solved. There is no reason your website and Instagram profile cannot be easily integrated so that website visitors discover and begin following your Instagram efforts. As a marketer, this barrier being removed is a huge advantage. It acts like a bridge from the old world of computer-based visitors to the new world of smartphone-based visitors. Your job is to consider all the ways you can get your tribe to walk back and forth across the bridge. You want to be fully relevant in the mobile context. In the near future, mobile marketing tactics and plans will become more prominent as computer-based marketing tactics begin to fade.

Two Paths, Two Experiences

The smartphone app version of Instagram will drive mobile traffic to your website whether your site is ready to be viewed on a mobile device or not. How does this happen? When Instagram users view your images via the smartphone app and they look at your Instagram profile, they will see your website URL as a clickable link. When they click it, they are taken to your website on their phones. So it stands to reason that the more Instagram followers you have, the more mobile visitors you'll have, too. If your website is not designed well for a mobile user experience, then you should work hard to get it up to speed.

The website profile version of your Instagram account is designed for computer users and will drive traffic back to your website via a traditional browser-based experience. So you have two paths and two different user experiences—one mobile and one computer based.

Ready for a Mobile User Experience?

According to research done by GoDaddy.com, 20 percent of Internet traffic comes from mobile devices, and that number is climbing quickly. It will not stop, because the truth is, the Internet experience is shifting to a mobile device experience. According to the Pew Internet & American Life Project, a full 50 percent of U.S. adults have a smartphone, and that number is growing. Google has reported that 80 percent of smartphone users look to purchase products on their phones. So mobile is the next wave of the Internet user experience.

It can be overwhelming to think about social changes like the shift to mobile. As marketers, we cannot lament all the hard work and effort we put into preparing our sites for computer-based visitors. All we can do is simply acknowledge that the mobile browsing experience is coming at us like a wave of user activity and expectation and prepare our online marketing initiatives accordingly.

Once we resolve to embrace the shift to mobile and decide to ramp up our efforts to meet the challenge, we can start to see real benefits. As with all other major societal shifts, the marketers that ride the wave will see the greatest benefits. Navigating the shift to a mobile user experience could be the competitive advantage you've been waiting for to gain market share. Is your competition as prepared to "go mobile" as you are? Work hard to jump out to an early lead on mobile devices and watch how it will improve your business results.

Computer-based Internet browsing will be around for a very long time, so the way our websites look via Internet Explorer, Safari, Chrome, and Firefox still matters a great deal. But we must add on a new layer of understanding, effort, and tactics so we can effectively market our products and services to mobile visitors.

Your Website's Primary Purpose

Before we can work to drive traffic to your website, we need to ensure that it is focused on one primary purpose. Most likely, that purpose is to sell products, but it might also be to capture prospects' e-mail addresses or provide them with content so you can make advertising revenue. Whatever the purpose of your website, you need to work hard to ensure that it is optimized for that activity.

Your Website's Primary Method

Part of the optimization process is to ask a related question, *What is your website's primary method?* You can have a singular purpose, but if the method to achieve that purpose is wrong, underpowered, or poorly executed, then your ability to achieve the purpose is going to be significantly hindered. For example, a website designed to capture e-mail addresses doesn't need to have tons of content. It needs to have one compelling reason for the prospect to submit his or her e-mail address. Usually that takes the form of a free gift.

Your Website's Primary Metric

Once you know your websites' primary purpose and primary method, you can determine your website's primary metric. Here are the two most common primary metrics:

1. If your website exists to make sales, then the metric is *revenue per visitor*, or the value per visitor. Imagine, for example, that in one month you have 10,000 unique visitors and you sell $10,000 worth of product on your website. Your revenue per visitor is $1. For every visitor that comes to your site, you can expect to earn $1.

2. If your website exists to capture e-mail addresses, then the metric is *names per visitor*. If in one month you have 10,000 unique visitors and you add 1,000 names to your e-mail address list, then your metric is 10:1—which means 10 visitors for every 1 name that you capture.

Lessons from Liberty Jane Patterns

On one of our company's websites, http://www.libertyjanepatterns .com, we saw mobile traffic grow from 6,700 visits in July 2012 to over 16,000 visits in December of that same year. That is a massive jump. We believe part of that is likely due to our work on Instagram. That traffic, when combined over a six-month period, added up to 57,000 visits. It represents 17.6 percent of the total traffic coming to the site. So 17.6 percent of our visitors were having a mobile viewing experience.

What devices were they using? During that six-month time period, 58 percent of our mobile visitors were viewing our site via an iPad, 21 percent were viewing the site from an iPhone, and 3 percent were viewing the site from an iPod Touch. Remarkably, the remaining 18 percent of mobile visitors viewed our site from one of 395 other devices. None of those devices drove more than 2 percent of the overall traffic, but together they added up to a significant amount. The 395 devices were both tablet and smartphone products from companies you're probably familiar with. The top 10 names after Apple were:

- Samsung

- Sony

- Motorola

- HTC

- Toshiba

- Acer

- Google

- Dell

- Kindle Fire

- Nook Tablet

As you can see from Figure 14.1, the visitors to our website from mobile devices viewed fewer pages, stayed on the site a shorter amount of time, and had a higher bounce rate than our computer-based visitors. All these stats tell us one thing: we need to do a better job adapting our website for the mobile user.

What is even more alarming about our website's mobile visitor statistics is that 54 percent of the visitors from mobile devices were new visitors to our site, a higher percentage than for our overall site average. So more new visitors are coming from mobile devices to our site than from computers, but they are having a worse experience. As you might

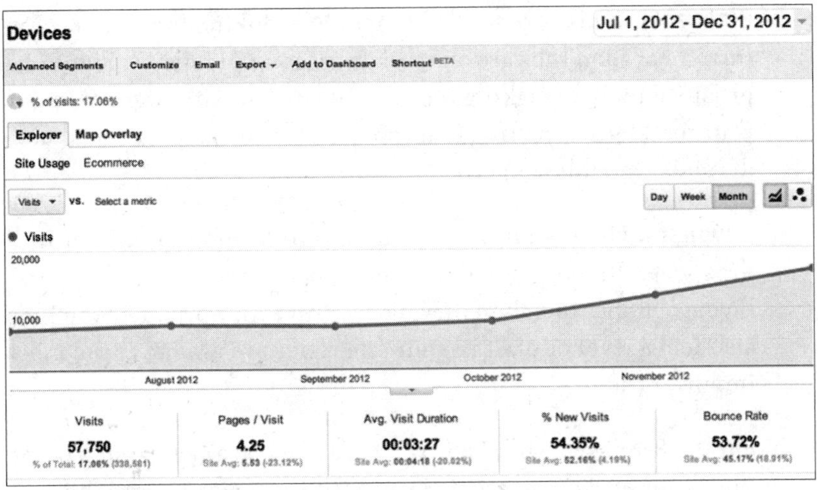

Figure 14.1 The Google Analytics for http://www.libertyjanepatterns.com shows that 17 percent of visits are from mobile devices.

guess, as we did the research for this chapter and looked at our own website statistics related to mobile users, a lightbulb went off—we need to be better at designing our site for a mobile user experience. What are your website statistics telling you?

Think Funnel

One way to improve your website's primary metric is to think in terms of a classic sales funnel. If your goal is to sell on your site, then consider each step in the sales cycle like a ring in a funnel. Your goal is to make the funnel as efficient as possible at advancing the prospect toward the next step. A classic sales funnel for e-commerce work might include these steps:

1. **Target market.** This is your ideal customer. These are the people on Instagram that you so carefully identified and followed. Your goal is to expose them to your brand or products and pique their interest by using the AIDA model.

2. **Visitors.** When these ideal customers visit your website, you've achieved a new milestone. You want them to have an instant love affair with your brand.

3. **Prospects.** If visitors find what they are looking for and become intrigued, then they are on track to be good prospects. Signs of a prospect include making repeat visits to your site, signing up for your newsletter, visiting multiple pages, visiting your social media sites, and following you.

4. **Shoppers.** Once visitors become familiar enough to turn into prospects, then the next step is to convert them into shoppers. If you've done this, then they like you and your product, and they also feel a level of trust in your site. They are almost at the most important step.

5. **Buyers.** People who buy from you have reached a critical step in the sales funnel. They entrusted you with their money, and they are trusting you to fulfill your promise to deliver the goods. Their positive experience will set the stage for them to make it into the next level, a highly prized group of people.

6. **Customers.** Repeat customers are the lifeblood of almost every business. Your goal is to turn the one-time buyer into the repeat customer.

7. **Raving fans.** Your most intense, passionate, and loyal customers are frequently referred to as your raving fans. These are the people you dream about getting—the people who buy the most, provide fantastic word-of-mouth referrals, leave raving online reviews, and generally work hard to promote your company.

Traffic Conversion and Analysis

One way to begin to understand your customer activity is to use Google Analytics or another analytics package. Your website traffic will begin to be more decipherable by carefully looking at the stats. To analyze your Instagram followers, you can use Statigram, a site we'll discuss in more detail later in the book. By looking at your Instagram followers on Statigram and your website visitors via Google Analytics, you start to get a good understanding of your smartphone users' behavior.

Integrating Instagram into Your Site

There are many practical ways to integrate Instagram into your site. Integrating your images into your website can provide nice visual content that is being updated frequently, and it will make the transition from your site to Instagram seamless and unintimidating, even for visitors who have never heard of Instagram. It also allows your visitors to easily find you on Instagram. Let's review the options together.

RSS

Your Instagram profile is designed to allow for Real Simple Syndication, or RSS. You can use an RSS feed for either a hashtag or a user profile. The RSS feed for a hashtag is http://instagr.am/tags/NAMEOF HASHTAG/feed/recent.rss. An Instagram RSS feed for a user profile is http://instagram.com/USERNAME/feed.

Open API

Instagram has an open application programming interface (API), which means that if you have a competent webmaster or want to hire one, you can fully integrate your Instagram photos into your website. You can, for example, have a "pictures" page that presents your Instagram images in a feed similar to what you'd experience on a phone.

Wordpress Options

Widgets exist to integrate your Instagram images into your WordPress .org-based website. There are lots of options to choose from in the widget area of your WordPress site. If you're a WordPress.org user, simply search in the widgets area within your site to find and add useful Instagram functionality.

Unfortunately, as of the time of this writing, there was no such widget available for WordPress.com sites. However, a user hack exists to allow you to display a hashtag feed on your WordPress.com website. Simply use the Flickr widget and include your Instagram hashtag RSS feed as described above, such as http://instagr.am/tags/mrjason

miles/feed/recent.rss. To see how this is used on my blog, visit http://www.marketingonpinterest.com and look for the Instagram feed in the right-hand column.

Social Sharing Buttons

The broad array of social sharing buttons that exists now includes Instagram. The most current social sharing buttons should likely include both Instagram and Pinterest as they are the hottest new social networks. Simply search for "Instagram social sharing buttons" to see a broad selection you can embed on your website. While you can't technically share anything on Instagram from a website, you can see and follow the company's Instagram profile by using these buttons.

Badges

A badge is a larger icon that indicates your Instagram user information. You can create it under your account at your Instagram website location. Then you insert the HTML code on your blog or website. There are five options, as shown in Figure 14.2.

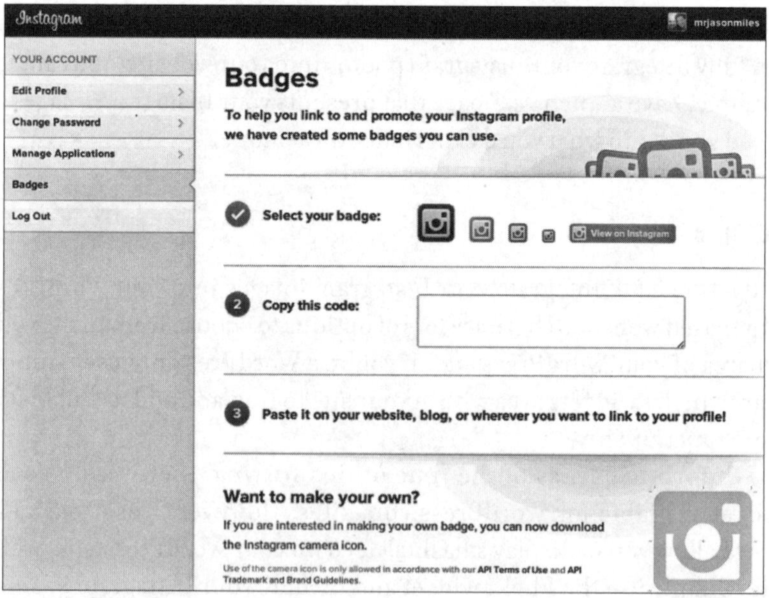

Figure 14.2 You can create a badge and add it to your website using the Instagram tool found on the website version of your profile.

New Methods

As Instagram develops as a platform, there will undoubtedly be new and better methods of integrating your website with the app. Stay current and continue to strive for a top-quality user experience for your mobile visitors.

THE SNAPSHOT

(1) You want to drive traffic from Instagram to your website, but you also want to drive traffic from your website to Instagram. (2) Calculate the revenue per visitor of your website and begin evaluating the worth of each visit. (3) Look at your analytics and determine the percentage of website visitors that are viewing your site from a mobile device. (4) Begin planning ways to optimize your website for the mobile user.

Instagram as Part of Your Social Strategy

*I*f you're like most marketers, when you heard that Instagram hit 100 million users, you thought, *Oh no, not another social network to deal with*. It's true; most of us are on social media overload. Something might need to give. Before we dive into the details of Instagram integration into your social media marketing mix, we should probably review a few of the basics to ensure Instagram is a good idea for your business.

In a recent interview, I was asked about our social media strategy at Liberty Jane Clothing, and the interviewer was shocked that I said, "We don't do Twitter." The truth is, you have to decide what social media platforms you're going to be on and which ones you're going to leave alone. As mentioned in Chapter 1, at our company our energy for social media efforts goes toward these platforms:

1. Facebook

2. YouTube

3. Pinterest

4. Instagram

If you're feeling overwhelmed by all the choices, then you should probably set aside some time to brainstorm your ideal social strategy. These questions come to mind:

1. What are you goals?

2. What are your talents and strengths?

3. What are your areas of weakness that need to be avoided?

4. What capacity do you have to manage multiple sites?

5. Are you willing to have a small and unpopular profile on any social platform?

6. Is there a social media platform that your target market uses more than the others?

The crucial questions for each social site are these: *Why are you on it? Do you have a clear goal or purpose for each site?*

POWER TIP

If you can't come up with a really good reason to be on a social media site, ask yourself whether you should give it up. If a platform doesn't work well for your business or your prospects, then don't feel bad about saying no.

You might wonder why we don't use Twitter for our business. Here is a brief rationale. We sell doll clothes, accessories, and sewing patterns to moms and daughters, as well as to collectors. They've never seemed that into Twitter. We asked our 14-year-old daughter if she wanted a Twitter account, and she said, "Eeww, no!" But she's on Pinterest and Instagram every day. We asked our 16-year-old son if his friends use Twitter, and he said, "No, Dad, that's just for following celebrities." These are adequate arguments for us to use to defend our nonuse. You might use Twitter and love it, and that's great for you. We each have to decide what is right for our circumstances and be comfortable defending our decisions. Time and mental bandwidth are finite, so sometimes you really do need to make sacrifices.

Go Big or Don't Go

Our approach to social media sites is fairly simply—either we like to go big, or we stay off the site entirely. So we'd rather not be on Twitter with 42 followers and very little activity occurring. Why go big or not go at all? Two reasons come to mind:

1. We are working hard to create the impression of a legitimate and "big" brand. We want to be respected. Having a tiny presence on a social site signals that you are not popular, at least on that site. We are eager to avoid that perception in any venue. We want the halo effect to influence our prospective customers when they encounter us on a social media site.

2. A big presence on a social site requires you to be fully engaged, which is good. When you have a small presence, work on the site seems to always get put on the to-do list that never gets done. Having a small presence makes it a small deal to you, and that is a recipe for mediocrity. If you find yourself saying, "We put that social media site on the back burner," then you know something is wrong. Be all in or get off the site.

Why Instagram Might Be Ideal for You

In our last book, *Pinterest Power*, we explained how on August 4, 2011, our Facebook fan page was shut down without warning or notice. The traffic from Facebook to our e-commerce site immediately stopped. Sales ebbed. Needless to say, we were freaked out. See, not only had we invested over four years in making comments, liking things, and sharing pictures and links; we had also worked hard to develop fans. Now called "likers," the fans on our fan page numbered roughly 12,000 at the time. These fans weren't acquired organically either. We had invested $400 to $600 per month for several years advertising our fan page. We had been good Facebook advertising customers, too—loyal, patient, and low maintenance.

So what happened? As it turns out, Facebook was trying to delete a huge collection of fake accounts, and it assumed ours was one of them. Apparently, it had something to do with millions of tween girls setting up Facebook accounts on behalf of their American Girl dolls and liking pages. Facebook bundled our account in with this group and hit delete. The good news was, after verifying that we were "real people," we were able to get our account reinstated.

The lesson we learned through that ordeal was really valuable. It's simple, and it might be a great reason for you to consider building an Instagram followership. When you operate on another company's website, you are not in control. It could be Facebook, eBay, Etsy, Pinterest, Instagram, YouTube, or Amazon. If you decide to use a company's services, be prepared for the company to shut down, close your account, suspend you, or seriously modify the TOS.

For this reason, our only security is in our e-mail list and the traffic we know we can drive to our own website. The other way in which we are safe is having our fans follow us on multiple social networks. It might sound paranoid, but it's a business safeguard that helps us sleep better at night. So how does this relate to Instagram and the other social media platforms? It's simple. There is safety in numbers.

When you have a large following on Facebook, for example, your wisest social strategy is to migrate as many of those users to another social media platform as quickly as possible. That way, you have two points of social media contact with them instead of just one. If anything happens to your original social site, you always have the secondary site. You want a social vineyard, not a social oak tree. Many companies are growing massive Facebook fan pages by spending a small fortune on advertising. I know of a company spending $2,000 a day on the Facebook advertising platform to advertise to get more likers. But the company has no other social media presence. What happens if Facebook goes the way of Myspace and closes down its account or changes the TOS in a way that makes the company uninterested in using the site? That is a dangerous place to be, and one we wouldn't recommend.

Are social networks going to last forever? Is it a "winner takes all" market? There doesn't seem to be any threat to Amazon in the e-commerce space or eBay in the auction space. Is Facebook the new Yellow Pages that will last for the next 50 years? Because there are so many unknowns, the only wise choice is to pick a few social networks that you can easily manage and truly enjoy, and then you work to build a presence on each with your customers. Ideally, you want to interact with them on multiple platforms. Let's look at how Instagram could be paired with the other top social networks.

Instagram and Facebook

Instagram and Facebook have a special relationship. In April 2012, Facebook purchased the company for a reported $1 billion. But beyond that business-related decision, Instagram's integration with Facebook is very straightforward, and as mentioned previously, the more you work to integrate the two sites, the better. Chances are insanely high that Facebook will continue to make integrating Instagram into its system a simple process. There are several options for integrating Instagram with your Facebook account, including:

- Adding Instagram images on a Facebook tab—the standard version. Adding the Instagram feed to your Facebook page is very simple. You can find out more about the setup steps at http://apps .facebook.com/instagram_feed/. The feed format features one picture at a time, as shown in Figure 15.1.

Figure 15.1 The feed layout for Instagram images in Facebook features one primary image at a time.

- Adding Instagram images on a Facebook tab—the grid version. The InstaTab app for Facebook allows for a grid-based view of your images within Facebook, as shown in Figure 15.2. This is a very nice look, and the app has three display modes. Set it up on your fan page by visiting http://apps.facebook.com/instatab/.

Figure 15.2 The grid layout for Instagram images in Facebook is a nice look.

Manually Sharing Photos to Your Facebook Fan Page

Within the Instagram app on your smartphone, you can easily share any of your pictures to Facebook seamlessly. To do this, you must have your Instagram account connected to your Facebook account on your smartphone. Here are the process steps:

1. Navigate to the Sharing settings under the Profile tab.

2. Tap on the Facebook button.

3. To have photos shared to your fan page, click the Share Photos To button and select the appropriate page.

Instagram and Pinterest

At first glance, you might think that Instagram and Pinterest are pretty much the same thing. But there are many differences in purpose, functionality, and manner of use. It might be accurate to say that Pinterest was the last great social network designed for the desktop experience and that Instagram was the first great social network designed for the smartphone experience. Pinterest has a beautiful desktop user experience, and Instagram has a beautiful smartphone user experience.

Pinterest is ideal for:

- Bookmarking and sharing great content from around the web

- Attracting visually oriented customers and prospects

- Creating collections of content, just as a librarian does, to refer to later and share with followers

- Driving massive referral traffic from your Pinterest profile to your website

- Displaying infographics, how-to images, and memes

Instagram is ideal for:

- Taking and editing beautiful photos from your phone

- Sharing your images with followers

- Attracting visually oriented prospects and followers

- Driving visitors from your Instagram profile to your e-commerce site, all from the users' smartphones

- Finding and following people that are interested in your niche, industry, or product

It is true that Pinterest has developed a very good app that allows you to have a nice Pinterest experience from your smartphone. And it is true that Instagram has developed a good website version that allows you to have a nice desktop experience. But the majority of Pinterest users access the site from a desktop, and Instagram is accessed primarily via smartphone.

To explore all the business benefits of Pinterest, be sure to pick up a copy of our bestselling book *Pinterest Power* or visit our blog at http://www.marketingonpinterest.com. The referral traffic available to your business from Pinterest is unprecedented. Not taking advantage of it is a serious mistake.

Instagram and Pinterest: Shared Images

The best scenario we've found for integrating the two social networks together is to take your Instagram images and upload them manually to Pinterest. I upload them to a pinboard called "My Instagram Pictures," but you could get much more creative than that and use Pinterest categories that make sense for your customers. Uploading your Instagram images to Pinterest lets your Pinterest followers know about your Instagram efforts. To fully leverage this opportunity, follow these steps:

1. Create pinboards on Pinterest that will hold your images. Be creative and make pinboards that you think will be of vital interest to your prospective followers.

2. From your smartphone, download the Instagram app.

3. After taking a picture and sharing it on Instagram, you'll automatically have a version of the edited photo in your camera roll.

4. Switch to the Pinterest app and choose to upload a picture.

5. Pick the edited Instagram image from your camera roll.

6. Choose the Pinterest pinboard that is most appropriate for the image and hit Upload.

7. You can also add a caption, such as "Follow me on Instagram @ mrjasonmiles."

Instagram and Twitter

It would appear that Instagram and Twitter are locked in a blood feud. In December 2012, Instagram disabled Twitter's ability to display Instagram images in people's Twitter feeds. Instead, the images can simply be shared as a clickable link. A week later, Twitter launched its own Instagramlike filter functionality.

If you are a long-time Twitter user and are starting to explore the idea of using Instagram, then you'll want to take note of this ongoing battle. Functionality and integration steps will likely change frequently as the sites decide what level of engagement they are willing to tolerate.

Migrating Followers

There are lots of ways to get users to shift from one social network and start following you on another. Let's look at some of the most common activities that can make that a reality. But don't be unrealistic; it is a long-term activity that will require patience and clear determination. Even after years of hard work, you'll probably never get 100 percent of your users on one site to follow you on a secondary site. But it's worth the effort.

The specific strategies you might employ include:

1. Using all the physical spaces provided on the sites to share your URL for the other sites. Most sites allow you to have at least one URL on your profile, similar to how Instagram does. Many provide enough space to include as many links as you want, like YouTube does. Always share your primary e-commerce site's URL if there is only space for one URL, but if there are spaces for more, be sure to include those too.

2. Sharing all your social networking addresses on your primary website. It's amazing how many website owners have not updated their home-page icons to include Pinterest and Instagram. That is the easiest way to cross-pollinate and gain new followers on those sites.

3. On Facebook and Twitter, sharing links to your Instagram and Pinterest images regularly.

4. On Facebook, adding the tab to display your Instagram images.

5. Using your e-mail newsletter to launch your newest social media site and invite people to follow you.

6. Creating a contest that you announce in your newsletter and on Facebook and Twitter, offering to do a special giveaway when you reach a certain number of followers on your newest social media site. For us at Liberty Jane, we offered to do a design contest when we reached 1,000 Instagram followers. It helped fuel our early growth.

A Social Snowball

The beautiful part of this type of multiplatform social media effort is that if you build a large and loyal following on one social media platform and you use these types of ongoing integration techniques, you can build a large and loyal following on a secondary site fairly easily. Then when you have two solid sites, it becomes even easier to build a strong presence on a third social site.

What's an example of this strategy? Let me illustrate by using our social network numbers. You might recall in Chapter 1, I referenced our social network results as follows:

- E-mail list: 19,000

- YouTube subscribers: 8,500 (1.5 million video views)

- Facebook fans: 23,000

- Pinterest followers: 4,800

- Instagram followers: 550

But I wrote that chapter five weeks ago, and when I did it, I rounded all the numbers down. In hindsight, if I had known I was going to look back and do some analysis, I would have documented the exact numbers. Sorry about that, but I hope you'll accept my analysis anyway. Obviously, in the last five weeks we've continued to grow. Each site grows in its own way, and we cross-pollinate as much as we can. Now, five weeks later, we have the following actual numbers:

- E-mail list: 21,978

- YouTube subscribers: 9,427 (1.7 million video views)

- Facebook fans: 25,647

- Pinterest followers: 5,778

- Instagram followers: 1,015

Notice that the percentage of growth is the largest on the sites that have the smallest number of users. In other words, doing this type of

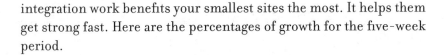

integration work benefits your smallest sites the most. It helps them get strong fast. Here are the percentages of growth for the five-week period.

- E-mail list: grew by 16 percent

- YouTube Subscribers: grew by 11 percent (video views grew by 14 percent)

- Facebook fans: grew by 12 percent

- Pinterest followers: grew by 20 percent

- Instagram followers: grew by 85 percent

Your Instagram work can be part of a vibrant and growing social media strategy. Take the time to think about how the entire system can work together and how Instagram can play a key part. Then focus on how you can leverage one social media site to build up the others. If I've made you curious about our growth, then you might enjoy checking our social media stats as you read this book to see how we've progressed from the time of this writing. I'd imagine the numbers are substantially higher.

THE SNAPSHOT

(1) Integrate Instagram into your social media mix. (2) Strive to have one primary use for each social media platform. (3) If a social media platform is a bad fit for your business, personal style, or prospects, then shut it down and don't look back. (4) Work hard to get your followers from your largest platform to begin following you on your smallest platform. You want to ensure multiple methods of engagement with each prospect or customer.

Chapter
16

Local Marketing with Instagram

Strengthening local marketing efforts via social media is a hot topic. And the good news is that the tools and techniques for integrating rich media into your local marketing efforts have never been better. In this chapter, we'll look at how local businesses and nonprofits can leverage the power of Instagram to make a deeper impact within their communities.

Isn't it about time the Web 2.0 revolution focused on local business? When the World Wide Web came out, it provided the opportunity for you to connect with people who shared similar interests with you but who might be separated by a vast distance. These affinity-based sites and communities changed our lives. But are you any closer to interesting people in your local community?

The Migration to Local Marketing

The period of affinity-based social media was really from 2004 to 2010. The large-scale platforms that connected people according to their similarities were the "killer apps" of the Web 2.0 movement. Myspace was the first commercial hit focused primarily on music. It started in August 2003. Facebook was started in February 2004, and although it seemed to be a runner-up for the first few years, it eventually caught and surpassed Myspace. YouTube launched in February 2005. Twitter launched in March 2006. Each of these sites was affinity or function based, without deliberate emphasis on strengthening local connections. They weren't bad for local marketers, but they weren't designed for them either.

But the emphasis began to shift in 2010 with the breakout success of the Foursquare app, the social network that promised to connect people with businesses. It technically started in March 2009, but as with most things, people didn't understand the gravity of the shift in thinking that it represented until sometime in 2010.

The current emphasis is to connect people by geography as well as affinity. Instagram plays in this space brilliantly, working to connect people by interests and by locations. Local businesses have an opportunity to enhance their interaction with their community in a new and exciting way using Instagram. Let's look at the ways local businesses can leverage the local nature of Instagram.

The Two Tools Available for Local Marketers

At a very high level, there are just two tools for which you can use Instagram to engage locally. First, you can use location-based information, which is a function of a smartphone's GPS technology. Or you can use hashtags, which don't technically relate to a location, but they can relate to anything you want, including an event or special location.

Six Ways to Engage Locally with Instagram

The two tools—location-based information and hashtags—provide an opportunity for countless engagement tactics for the creative marketer. Let's look at six tactics that are commonly used today.

1. Geotagging Your Business

Instagram was updated in 2012 to include location-centric information so that each of your pictures can be plotted on a map (see Figure 16.1). The geographic information can be shared by users, if they wish, by toggling the Photo Map function on or off on their Home tab. If the Photo Map feature is enabled, then Instagrammers can add their business locations to their image information as they are finalizing their pictures.

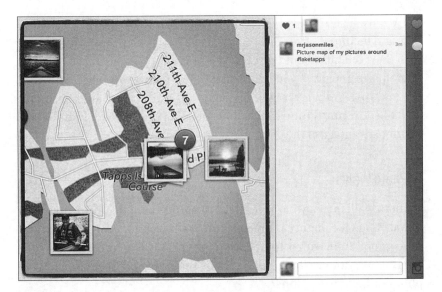

Figure 16.1 Your photo map visually represents the geotag data. You can choose to name a location as well. I frequently choose Tapps Island Golf Course as the named location, since it's near the dock where I like to take pictures.

POWER TIP

Instagram depends on the Foursquare location database to provide recommended names for users to "name this location" as they share an image. If you need to modify your businesses information, log in to Foursquare.com and clarify your company's information.

To ensure that your business address and name are properly displayed on Instagram in the Name This Location section, you need to tag your business as you're uploading an image onto Instagram and see what information is presented. If you don't like the way the information is presented, then you can update it. All the business and location information that is displayed in the search results on Instagram comes from the Foursquare location database. To modify it, you must join Foursquare, go to the Check-In tab, search for the place you want, and then tap Add This Place.

We are just in the very early days of utilizing geotags for local marketing. The initial effort is simply to have prospective customers share with their friends about their interactions with your business. And the Foursquare app gives you additional functionality to engage with customers. Instagram leveraged the Foursquare location database, and it won't be long until future apps and social media sites are built to take further advantage of the data.

2. Photo Walks

A photo walk is just what you might imagine—people joining together to walk and take pictures. You meet up, walk around, take pictures, and have a good time with other photographers. You can find out more details about photo walks in your area by searching on http://worldwide photowalk.com/locations/.

Once you experience a photo walk, you can plan to organize one for your area, if it makes sense for your business. Most photo walks are best done in an area that is tourist focused, say, downtown in a big city or in a getaway or vacation spot. If you're running a business in one of those spots, then you can coordinate photo walks that start and stop at your establishment. It's an easy way to meet new prospective customers.

MONETIZATION STRATEGY #8

Regularly conduct photo walks in your community and advertise them in the local newspaper with the headline "New in Town? Come on a Photo Walk with Us." Building a relationship with people who are just moving into your area gives you an advantage over your competition.

3. In-Event Sharing

Any time you conduct an activity like a special event, fund-raiser, summer picnic, or even just a regular Sunday church service, you have the opportunity to include participants in the event by having them share images using a hashtag. Simply announce the hashtag in your promotional materials and let the crowd do the rest.

4. Social Rally

Do you need to mobilize a special event like a rally, sporting event, or concert? A special hashtag will allow all the participants to tag their photos so they can be shared by all. Your job is to simply create the hashtag.

5. Local Contests

Lots of photo contests can be done online in various formats. But there isn't any reason why a contest cannot be done locally, too. The elements are the same, including:

- Launching your contest with a specific call to action.

- Having a clear set of rules and guidelines posted online, including a clear start date and end date.

- Driving user behavior toward a goal that helps share your brand's story and promotes your work.

- Making the activity fun and engaging.

- Making entering easy, for example, "To enter, simply include the hashtag #Contest1234."

- Having an amazing prize. People will do an incredible amount of work for a prize that they highly covet. Think through how your prizes can be unique and exciting for people who like your brand.

6. Coupons and Special Offers

We've mentioned our dislike of discounts in a previous chapter, but that doesn't mean you can't use Instagram to promote special offers. If you're a local business, give away a free item on a certain day and time. See how powerful your Instagram advertising can get. Learn to use Instagram for this type of direct marketing and integrate it into your business calendar. Launching a new product? Give away a secondary item for free at the same time to draw a large crowd. Staying open later in the summer? Give away a special gift for people who visit in the last hour of your new schedule each day for the first week.

Restaurants and Instagram

When the owners of Comodo, a new restaurant in New York City, noticed that many of their patrons were taking Instagram photos of their meals, the creative owners decided to make it even easier for customers to use Instagram in the restaurant. They created the hashtag #Comodomenu and shared it at the bottom of the physical menu. That simple action strengthened and guided the behavior of their customers.

Now when guests sit down to order a meal, they can search quickly on Instagram for that hashtag and see a picture of the food from a prior guest's perspective. The menu not only lets customers see what they are going to get, but also allows them to pass on the tradition by sharing a picture of their menu items when they arrive at the table. Of course, all those guests' Instagram followers also see it and are influenced to visit Comodo, too.

> **MONETIZATION STRATEGY #9**
>
> Publish a hashtag along with your menu, catalog, price tag, or online product description to tell your customers where to find and share product images. Giving them more information about a product before they buy is always a good idea.

Up Close with United Generation Youth Ministry

United Generation is the high school and college program at Puyallup Foursquare Church. It is a small-town church making a really big impact. Don't be confused by the name; it has nothing to do with the Foursquare app discussed previously in this chapter. The church had over 8,000 people in attendance last Easter and integrates social media into its work in several ways. As you can see from Figure 16.2, the youth ministry uses Instagram.

I asked Erika Blanco, United Generation's social media team leader, how she became familiar with Instagram. She said:

> Like many people with an interest in technology, I frequently find myself investigating new platforms and testing their

Figure 16.2 United Generation Youth Ministry is a ministry of Puyallup Foursquare Church. No, it is not associated with the Foursquare app mentioned previously in this chapter.

usability. Who wants to be left behind when the next big thing comes along? Most stay on my phone and get deleted after about six months, but Instagram was much different. It instantly became my favorite social media platform because of its simplicity and visual strength. As a new mom, it was my digital photo album. My son's first smile, first steps, and all else were easily snapped, shared, and seen by our family and friends.

Erika's personal use of Instagram led to the church team adopting it for its work with local teens as well. The team regularly ministers to over 1,000 teenagers a week. When I asked her how that came about, she told me:

When we love something in our personal lives, we are eager to integrate it into our church communications strategy. Our youth (high school and college) ministries were the first to use Instagram. This audience is more resilient to change and also more technologically literate. The value was instantly clear—visual imagery. In our communications department, we are constantly editing what we are doing by "cutting the words in half, and then in half again." Our audience is familiar with media and marketing by mainstream companies who spend billions every year to create the perfect image. To compete with an attention span that is conditioned to viewing images and quick messages, we are constantly trying to show rather than explain our message. Instagram is perfect for that strategy.

The United Generation team members have a solid set of action steps to accomplish their Instagram work. Here is how they describe it:

> We have a photography team, a social media team, and a graphics team that all partner together. This team is constantly expanding and giving creative people an outlet. Multiple people managing one account has been the most successful strategy for us.
>
> In an effort to improve our quality of pictures as well as promote the creative community, we have a rotation of volunteer photographers that shoot our services, events, and meetings. They send us their best edits and we post. The photographers have included Daniel Dillard, Jeff Marsh, Phu Nguyen, Caroline Lindsley, Nicole Gibbons, and many others.

I asked Erika what advice she'd have for new Instagram users, if she could boil down the United Generation Youth Ministry's experiences, and she suggested the following:

1. With every post keep in mind: if I were reading this without any context, would I . . .
   a. Know what's going on?
   b. Feel involved or included?
   c. Be compelled to join?

2. Be mindful to engage beyond your post. Just because you posted it doesn't mean that everyone knows about it!

3. Don't assume people know what you are posting. We have found that a post with little context is worse than posting nothing at all.

4. Keep it clear.

5. Keep it consistent.

6. Leave them wanting more.

THE SNAPSHOT

(1) Instagram is ideal for cultivating local prospects, customers, fans, and followers. (2) Use both hashtags and geotags to connect people to your business, church, or service. (3) Use Instagram to engage participants in events. (4) Make sure your business is listed properly in the Foursquare location database. (5) Build a team of volunteers to help you manage your Instagram efforts.

Part 6

TOOLS FOR LEVERAGING YOUR INSTAGRAM EXPERIENCE

Complementary Apps and Websites

An ecosystem of industrial-strength tools has grown up quickly in support of the Instagram user experience. Companies have created both apps and websites that help leverage and extend the work of Instagrammers. While many of these are intended for the general public, as a marketer, you can use these tools to help enhance your marketing efforts in several exciting ways. You even have the opportunity to use the tools to create new product opportunities. The types of tools include:

- Tools that help you view Instagram on a computer desktop

- Tools that help you view Instagram on an iPad

- Tools that help you turn Instagram images into physical products

- Tools that help you sell your Instagram work

- Tools that help you management your Instagram photos

- Tools that help you leverage the geotag information

- Tools that help manage the hashtag and follower management process

- Tools that help you integrate Instagram with other sites

- Tools that help you improve your photography

- Tools that help provide personal productivity

In this chapter, we'll look at complementary apps that help make Instagram that much better. In the next chapter, we'll look at apps specifically designed to help you manage and analyze the data being generated by Instagram interactions.

Desktop Viewers

The early third-party tools created in support of Instagram focused on trying to compensate for the fact that Instagram had no desktop viewer. But in late 2012, Instagram launched its own desktop profile system, and so the need for third-party viewers is declining. While these tools are no longer crucial, many of them have very nice functionality and are worth looking into.

- **Statigram.** The most popular of the third-party web viewing tools. In addition to having useful functionality related to managing your Instagram account, it also provides analytics. We'll look at the analytics functions in the next chapter.

- **Webstagram.** Like Statigram, a web viewer with the functionality you expect from the Instagram application. Plus you get additional features not found on Instagram.

- **Carousel**. A nice Instagram app for Macs. This is probably the most stylish desktop web viewer for the Mac. It displays your images in a very elegant way.

- **INK361.** A desktop viewer for browsing, liking, and commenting on Instagram images. This provider also has a nice collection of apps that do various things. Check the Tools tab to see what new apps the company has come up with to support Instagram.

- **Followgram.** Another desktop viewer for browsing, liking, and commenting on Instagram images.

- **Gramfeed.** Another desktop viewer for browsing, liking, and commenting on Instagram images.

- **Extragram.** And another desktop viewer for browsing, liking, and commenting on Instagram images. This tool is useful, but the functions are not as strong as Webstagram's.

- **Instac.at.** A web application to search for relevant Instagram images based on hashtags and keywords.

- **Insta-great.** A web application that allows you to take your Instagram photos and see them presented in a horizontal timeline.

iPad Tools

To date, there is not an official Instagram viewer or app for the iPad. But there are options you can use. If you want to use the official Instagram app on your iPad, then you can simply download and run the iPhone app, and the app will display in a small window. But visually, that is not ideal, as it doesn't take advantage of the large-format screen. So several options exist to use Instagram on the iPad, including:

- **Instagallery.** A browsing tool for your iPhone or iPad. When you hit the app's Play button, it will start a slide show and scroll through the photos for you.

- **Padgram.** A browsing tool for your iPad that allows for much of the functionality of the iPhone version.

- **Flipboard.** A truly great app. When you install Flipboard and connect your social media accounts, it creates a magazine-style layout using all your information. It turns your iPad into a magazine featuring you and your friends. You can connect Instagram as one of the possible display options, as well as Facebook, LinkedIn, Twitter, and more. This app is very engaging and presents your social media content in a different visual format than you are accustomed to seeing. I highly recommend Flipboard.

From Images to Physical Products

There is a growing collection of apps and services that will turn your Instagram images into physical products. This means that your Instagram work can transcend being a social media tool and can actually be used as a physical product with your customers and prospects. What can you do with the help of these apps? Consider the following:

1. Turn your Instagram images into postcards that you use in your cultivation and relationship-building efforts.

2. Create a calendar out of your Instagram images and sell it.

3. Create stickers out of your Instagram images and include several free in each package that you send out. If your Instagram images are interesting to your target market, then a few free stickers would be appreciated. You could also use these as giveaway items at trade shows.

4. Create magnets out of your Instagram images and sell them on your website or give them away to your best customers.

5. Create beautiful coffee table–quality books and sell them. Or give one to your "customer of the year" or hold a contest and give one away.

The following apps will help you get these jobs done:

- **StickyGram.** Print Instagram images as magnets (see Figure 17.1). Who doesn't like refrigerator magnets?

- **Blurb.** Blurb books are beautifully finished. If you take the time to add your Instagram images with some nice quotes, you can get a finished product that is bookstore quality. Your customers will love it.

- **Instagoodies.** Make a book of stickers out of your Instagram images.

- **Printstagram.** Printstagram gives you the ability to print your Instagram photos. Options include mini-albums, posters, and stickers.

- **Postagram.** Turn your Instagram images into postcards.

- **ixxi.** ixxi is a decorative wall system based on your Instagram images. You select the style of system you want; then it is printed and delivered ready to be installed as high-end wall art. Get started at http://www.ixxidesign.com/ink361.

- **Instaprint.** Instaprint is a rentable physical printer designed specifically to support Instagram photos at parties and large-scale events! The device re-creates the nostalgia of the old-school Polaroid-style photos and lets your partygoers have a fun keepsake.

- **Instamaker.** Apply your Instagram photos to a wide collection of physical products including mugs, shirts, and even necklaces.

- **Calendagram.** Print your Instagram photos on a calendar.

- **Casetagram.** Want to make an iPhone case out of your Instagram images? Casetagram can help you make it happen.

Figure 17.1 The magnets from Stickygram turn out really nicely and come in a cool package. They come on a sheet that you peel apart.

Sales Management Platforms

Making physical products from your Instagram images is one thing; having a website that allows you to immediately set up a storefront shop and beginning selling to a community of buyers is another level altogether. Although at the time of this writing there is only one company in this category, it stands to reason that this will be a hot topic in the future, with many sites developing the tools to make this a reality. See how this works at:

- **ARTFLAKES.** ARTFLAKES allows you to print posters, art prints, canvas prints, gallery prints, greeting cards, and Instagram stickers. Additionally, you can set up your own storefront and sell your Instagram images in these formats. Monetize your Instagram images.

MONETIZATION STRATEGY #10

Set up an ARTFLAKES shop and start selling your Instagram images as canvas prints, posters, greeting cards, and more. If you have strong brand loyalty, it could turn into a vibrant new product line.

Photo Management Utilities

If you're worried that you might lose track of all your amazing Instagram images and you want a tool to quickly export them to your desktop, then you're in luck. Consider these options:

- **Instagram Downloader.** Wondering how you can manage your Instagram images off Instagram? This simple tool helps you download your Instagram images.

- **Instaport.** Similar to Instagram Downloader, Instaport is a downloading tool.

■ **Instarchive.** Similar to Instagram Downloader, Instarchive is a web tool that allows you to download all your Instagram images into a single folder on your desktop.

Geotag Mapping Utilities

If you're focused on images based on location, then you'll want to explore options for viewing the geotag data. While there are likely more options, we found the following site helpful:

■ **Instamap.** The Instamap app allows you to view your Instagram pictures using the geotagging information. You can also subscribe to geographic locations or hashtags and see the images as they get posted.

Hashtag and Follower Management Utilities

If you want to speed up your Instagram work, then consider utilities that help you manage the most time-consuming aspects of the site: the hashtag process and the follower management process. Fortunately there are sites that help you with both these issues. Consider these options:

■ **Instatag.** Wondering how to quickly manage hashtags so the process of adding them to photos is not slow and cumbersome? Instatag is a hashtag management tool. It is a quick way to tag your Instagram photos with the most popular and relevant hashtags.

■ **InstaFollow.** This follower management tool lets you see who is following you, who you follow that is not following you, and who is following you that you are not following. You can quickly unfollow people with this tool if you find that they are not following you.

POWER TIP

With InstaFollow, you can regularly unfollow people who are not following you back. Use this tool to ensure you have more followers than people you follow.

Integration Management Utilities

If you integrate your Instagram work into your website, Facebook fan page, and other locations, then chances are good that your existing customers and fans will migrate to your site to follow you on Instagram. As we've discussed in previous chapters, this is one of your wisest social media marketing moves. Get your fans and followers connected to you in multiple ways. To help you accomplish this goal, consider these tools:

- **Olapic.** Olapic provides an integration tool for putting user-generated photos on your website. This tool is particularly useful when you are trying to manage a contest that includes presenting images on your website.

- **Chute.** Similar to Olapic, Chute allows you to add user-generated images to your website. Get started at http://www.getchute.com/.

- **InstaFB.** Share your Instagram images to Facebook seamlessly and categorize them in folders.

Photo Editing Apps

You can edit your images right on your smartphone with a nice collection of photo editing apps. If you want to ensure your images look just right, then use one of these apps to check them and then upload them to Instagram.

- **Photoshop Express.** If you love Photoshop or Photoshop Elements, then you'll appreciate the Photoshop Express app. Not only is this app loaded with useful features, but it's free!

- **instaCap.** instaCap allows you to add captions to your Instagram images. The free version gives you quotes to add; the premium version allows you to type your own messages.

- **PolyFrame.** Need to create a collage? PolyFrame offers simple collage-style photo editing.

- **Squaready.** This app helps you get your Instagram images perfectly square, so no annoying black bars appear at the top or bottom.

- **Diptic.** Using this collage-style photo editing tool, you can include multiple images in one Instagram photo.

- **LensLight.** Interested in adding interesting lighting effects to your images? LensLight lets you add a nice collection of options.

- **Pixlr-o-matic.** With Pixlr-o-matic, you can choose from a nice collection of effects including sparkles and realistic looking rain. The filters available through this app are very good.

Personal Productivity

There are many tools being developed that help you integrate Instagram into your life in cool ways. These might not be strong for marketing purposes, but maybe they'll help you brighten your day and keep your Instagram work top of mind. Consider trying these tools:

- **MorningPics.** MorningPics is a web-based program that randomly chooses one of your Instagram images and sends it to you via e-mail. Relive those memories with MorningPics.

- **Momento.** Momento is a daily diary app that allows you to include Instagram images.

- **Screenstagram.** This is a web viewer that displays your and your friends' Instagram images in a Pinterest-style feed.

THE SNAPSHOT

(1) Third-party apps and websites can substantially improve your Instagram work. (2) Use them to effectively edit your images, manage your account, and integrate Instagram into your website and Facebook account. (3) Consider creating a collection of physical products based on your Instagram work for profit and customer cultivation purposes. (4) Use personal productivity apps to ensure you continue to enjoy your Instagram work.

Analyzing Your Instagram Work

*Y*our Instagram work can be optimized by using analytical tools. The good news is that there are several good tools to choose from, and more are being made all the time. These tools will help you dial in your Instagram sharing so that you can accomplish more in less time. What are the questions you might want to find answers to? Here is a short list:

1. How do I increase my number of followers more quickly?

2. What time of the day should I post my images so they get liked a lot?

3. What day of the week should I post my images so they get liked a lot?

4. What kinds of images are most popular with my audience?

5. How many people are coming from Instagram to my website?

6. Which hashtags should I use?

7. How many visitors to my website are viewing it on a mobile device?

Analytics can answer all these questions and more. As it turns out, the degree to which people engage with your Instagram content is highly dependent on factors that you can control. You've got to learn what those factors are and how to align your Instagram work with them to effectively leverage your time on the site.

A Goal-Oriented Approach

There is no reason to look at analytics if you don't have any goals. So it makes sense to start by being very clear about your goals for success on Instagram. Earlier in the book, we suggested striving for 1,000 followers as your first goal. We hope you've taken up that challenge. Here are examples of goals we might recommend:

1. I want to add 1,000 followers as quickly as possible.

2. I want to convert a lot of my existing Facebook fans, Twitter followers, and e-mail newsletter subscribers to following me on Instagram.

3. I want to get new customers to visit my website from Instagram.

4. I want to create buzz and enthusiasm for my business by using hashtags.

5. I want to drive purchasing behavior from Instagram and prove it is effective.

6. I want to make my brand more appealing using Instagram.

In this chapter, we'll cover several of the tools available to help us with the effort of analysis and optimization. We'll also examine how to use the tools to answer your questions and reach your goals. There is a simple rule of thumb that I always like to use: *observation, organization, optimization.* First we observe the concept, then we organize ourselves to apply it to our business, and then we do the optimization.

Analytics Tools

As with any platform, the tools available to support Instagram business users are always changing. This collection is certainly not complete, but it represents the popular options. The best way I've found to keep up-to-date is to follow the great site TechCrunch. It constantly reports on new ventures and explains how the technology industry is shifting. So let's look at a few of the popular tools that will help get the analytical job done.

Google Analytics

Your Google Analytics (GA) account can provide a very solid collection of data points related to mobile traffic. The first and most basic question about Instagram is, *How many people come from Instagram to my website, and what do they do?* Sadly, GA doesn't easily provide the answer, but it does shed light on it indirectly. Let's look at a few ways it does that.

Mobile Users Data

Your GA account information listed under the Mobile tab provides a wide collection of information about your mobile users' experience. You can see the number of visits, number of page views, average visit duration, percentage of new visitors, bounce rate, and more.

As shown in Figure 18.1, we had 87,000 mobile visitors to http://www.libertyjanepatterns.com in 2012, with significant growth occurring in the last three months. What can we learn from the information in Figure 18.1? Here are a few lessons:

1. Mobile traffic for the year was 14 percent of our site's total traffic. For the last three months, the mobile traffic averaged over 18 percent, with the trendline clearly growing.

2. Mobile visitors view one less page on average than desktop users.

3. Mobile visitors spend almost 30 fewer seconds on the site than desktop users.

4. There are more new visitors to the site coming from mobile devices than there are from desktop computers. It's a slight difference, but that is an interesting statistic.

5. The bounce rate for mobile users is 16 percent higher than the site average.

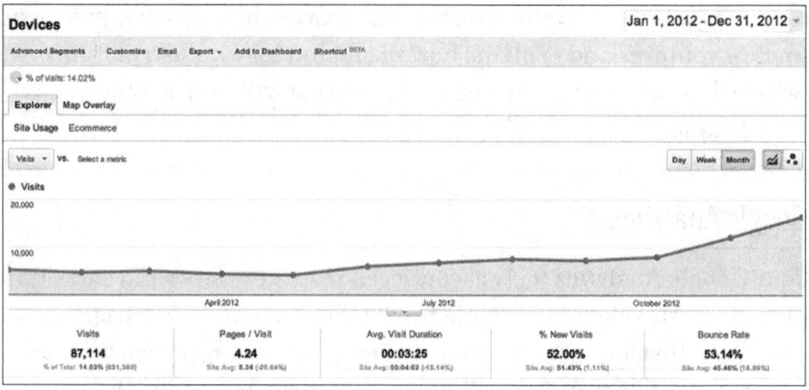

Figure 18.1 Looking at the mobile traffic in GA lets you know how many of your website's visitors are accessing the site on a mobile device.

Mobile Device Data

GA also provides insight into the various types of mobile devices and how significant a part they play in your traffic. Instagram can be used on an iPhone, iPad, or Android-based phone, so you can't tell for sure if the traffic coming from these devices was from Instagram or not, but it's still helpful to know the types of devices being used. In the future, it might certainly be the case that GA provides additional details related to Instagram and the devices used.

In January 2012, we found that 260 different mobile devices were used to access http://www.libertyjanepatterns.com. You can readily see from Figure 18.2 that the top device was the iPad, followed by the iPhone and then the iPod.

Mobile Device Info	Visits	Pages / Visit	Avg. Visit Duration	% New Visits	Bounce Rate
1. Apple iPad	10,729	5.38	00:04:06	47.46%	47.43%
2. Apple iPhone	3,483	2.99	00:02:33	60.12%	63.59%
3. Apple iPod	754	4.55	00:04:03	50.80%	49.87%
4. (not set)	440	5.95	00:04:47	41.14%	53.86%
5. Google Nexus 7	153	5.59	00:03:24	50.33%	54.90%
6. Samsung GT-P5113 Galaxy Tab 2 10.1 WiFi	125	3.93	00:03:51	37.60%	70.40%
7. Samsung GT-P3113 Galaxy Tab 2 7.0	107	3.92	00:03:15	42.06%	60.75%
8. Motorola MOTXT912B Droid Razr 4G	91	4.99	00:03:52	57.14%	58.24%
9. Samsung GT-P7510 Galaxy Tab 10.1	80	4.32	00:03:34	26.25%	46.25%
10. Amazon Kindle Fire Kindle Fire	74	2.12	00:03:55	28.38%	58.11%

Figure 18.2 Looking at the type of mobile device used to access your website will provide answers related to the type of experience your visitors are having.

POWER TIP

Your website traffic is migrating to mobile devices at an astonishing rate, even if you're not aware of it yet. It's time to start looking into it and asking the hard question, *How does your website work for mobile device users?*

The primary question to ask when looking at your mobile users' data is whether those users are having a good experience relative to your desktop users. You can determine this by looking at the average results by device and then comparing them with your site average. Each website will be different; as you can see in Figure 18.2, our mobile users stay on the site the longest when accessing it from an iPad.

There are advanced functions available in GA that will allow you to have better visibility into your Instagram traffic, but the basic functions don't readily show these results. If you're fortunate enough to have a GA guru on your team, then a top priority will be to optimize for this purpose. But GA isn't the only tool available to us. Let's look at the sites dedicated to helping parse the Instagram data.

Bitly

Bitly (formerly Bit.ly) is a service that helps shorten URLs, and if you use it creatively, then you can enhance your Instagram analytics. While the site isn't designed to specifically assist with Instagram, its functionality serves a good purpose that is lacking in GA. Let's look at the two meaningful statistical elements we can learn from using Bitly:

- **Visitors from Instagram.** If you use a Bitly short URL and place it on your Instagram profile instead of your regular URL, then you can track the traffic coming out of Instagram and onto your website. You do that by making a Bitly short link that points to your e-commerce site; then in Instagram you use the Bitly link instead of your website. That allows all the clicks that occur from Instagram to be tracked. In Figure 18.3, you can see our traffic results for a recent 24-hour period.

■ **Mobile versus website traffic.** If you place the Bitly short code on your Instagram profile, then people who are visiting your profile from a desktop and click on the URL will show up in the Bitly reports separately from people who are accessing your Instagram account from a mobile device. As shown in Figure 18.4, you can distinguish between people who visited from a desktop and from a mobile device. In our recent example, 10 percent of the visitors were from Instagram.com (the desktop version of the application) versus 90 percent who visited from a mobile device. Bitly doesn't distinguish between an iPad user and an iPhone user; it includes all of them under the Email Clients, IM, AIR Apps, and Direct category.

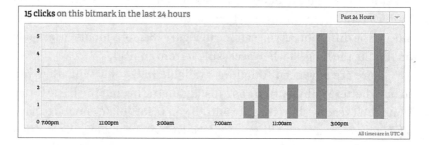

Figure 18.3 With a Bitly short URL on your Instagram profile, you can track the clicks that come through your Instagram account.

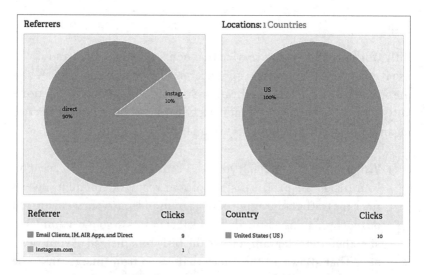

Figure 18.4 On Bitly you can distinguish between people visiting from a mobile device and those coming from a desktop.

Statigram

Statigram is a very useful site for understanding the metrics of your Instagram use. It provides the statistical information you're probably looking for related to your Instagram account performance. It also provides account management tools, so you can work on your Instagram account right through Statigram's desktop interface. You can do things like commenting, liking, and following.

- **Follower growth.** Viewing the details related to your follower growth is easy in Statigram. In the Community section of the analytics, you can see your follower growth as well as the relationship you have with the followers (see Figure 18.5).

- **Engaging content.** Statigram provides useful information about the volume of images you share, the types of filters you use, the tags you use, and the day and hour you post images. This type of information can be helpful in cases where you're struggling to connect with people.

- **Follower engagement.** Statigram tells you about the level of engagement occurring with your content, including which images are liked, which ones are commented on, which users engage the most, and whether your comments and likes come from followers

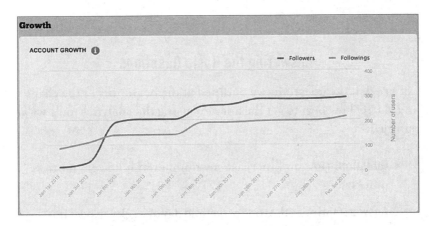

Figure 18.5 On Statigram you can track your follower growth rate and other account-related metrics.

or nonfollowers. You can see summary information about how your Instagram work is being received.

- **Optimization.** Statigram documents your typical behavior and habits and allows you to see them with a bird's-eye view (see Figure 18.6). It lets you see the impact of your filters and hashtags.

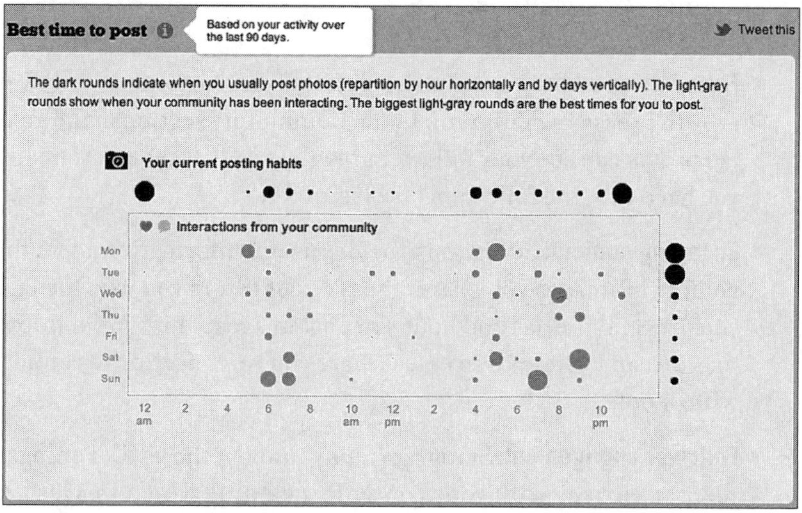

Figure 18.6 Statigram helps you understand when you post versus when your followers are most actively interacting with your content. Aligning the two helps you optimize responses.

Answering the Basic Questions

Let's revisit the questions we outlined at the beginning of the chapter and clarify how best to get the answers using the analytics tools we've outlined.

- **Question:** How do I increase my number of followers more quickly?

  Answer: Optimize the time of day and day of week you post images by using the Statigram optimization features. Also look at the engagement data in Statigram. Getting lots of followers happens faster when you have a lot of content that people are liking feverishly. Create content that will resonate with your audience. As a side note, don't forget to simply like 100 images from people within your niche every day. That simple proactive act will boost your numbers very quickly.

- **Question:** What time of the day should I post my images so they get liked a lot?

  Answer: Look at your optimization data in Statigram and begin following the suggestions.

- **Question:** What day of the week should I post my images so they get liked a lot?

  Answer: As with the time-of-day question, simply look at the optimization data in Statigram and begin following the suggestions.

- **Question:** What kinds of images are most popular with my audience?

  Answer: Look at the Engagement data in Statigram.

- **Question:** How many people are coming from Instagram to my website?

  Answer: Set up a Bitly URL and place it on your Instagram profile. Then monitor the stats in Bitly. You'll learn about the usefulness of your profile link.

- **Question:** Which hashtags should I use?

  Answer: Look at the Tag Impact section on the Statigram Optimization tab. You'll see a comparison between the hashtags you're using and the best possible hashtags, plus you'll see a recommendation for which ones to focus on.

- **Question:** How many visitors to my website are viewing it on a mobile device?

Answer: Look at your GA in the Mobile section to see how many people come from each device and to see the total number of mobile users.

Reaching Data-Driven Goals

Now let's revisit the goals we outlined at the beginning of the chapter and clarify how best to achieve them using both the analytics referenced in this chapter and the strategies previously recommended in this book.

Goal #1.
I want to add 1,000 followers as quickly as possible.

Strategy #1

1. Invite all your Facebook fans, Twitter followers, and e-mail newsletter subscribers to follow you on Instagram. Ask them repeatedly over several months, without being repetitive or annoying.

2. Like 100 pictures a day from people who you know are interested in your niche.

3. Leave 10 comments a day on pictures from people in your niche or industry.

4. Follow people who are already following industry insiders in your niche.

5. Use hashtags relevant to your niche or industry.

6. Look at the analytics and determine how to optimize your postings.

Goal #2.
I want to convert a lot of my existing Facebook fans, Twitter followers, Pinterest followers, and e-mail newsletter subscribers to following me on Instagram.

Strategy #2

1. Follow the steps in Goal #1 above, and also do a contest in Instagram that you promote to your existing fans on your other social

media sites. In other words, reward them for following you on Instagram with the prospect of winning a cool prize.

2. Integrate your Instagram profile information onto all your other social media website profiles, such as YouTube, Pinterest, Twitter, and Facebook.

3. Use the Facebook fan page InstaTab for Instagram integration.

4. Post your Instagram images to Twitter, Facebook, and Pinterest.

Goal #3.
I want to get new customers to visit my website from Instagram.

Strategy #3

1. Hold a contest on Instagram that requires participants to use your business hashtag as a method of entry. Let them know that the images that are entered will be displayed on your website and that a winner will be picked from among the contestants.

2. Make sure your profile description is well written and clearly extends an invitation for people to visit your site.

3. Use a Bitly short URL to monitor your success at getting people to click through to your site from your Instagram profile.

4. Advertise a special offer on Instagram only, like free shipping for a limited time for people who buy something on your website.

Goal #4.
I want to create buzz and enthusiasm for my business by using hashtags.

Strategy #4

1. Create a contest using a special business-specific hashtag.

2. Remember to make your hashtags specific and not open to being easily hijacked.

3. Feature the images tagged with your hashtag on your website so people feel rewarded for doing it.

4. Leave a comment on the images that are tagged, thanking people for doing it.

5. Like the images tagged.

Goal #5.
I want to drive purchasing behavior from Instagram and prove it is effective.

Strategy #5

1. Use display ads that offer something for free and only publicize them on Instagram. Monitor the results through your shopping cart sales results or GA.

2. Do a visual product launch that is only mentioned on Instagram.

3. Choose a different product and use a similar visual product launch strategy that you only promote on Twitter or Facebook. Compare the results of the various campaigns.

Goal #6.
I want to make my brand more appealing using Instagram.

Strategy #6

1. Show behind-the-scenes pictures of your products, such as during the design and construction phases.

2. Show pictures of your team working together.

3. Show pictures of your product being used by prestigious people.

4. Show pictures of your company at big events, like trade shows and industry conferences.

5. Show pictures of your company engaged in charitable activities.

6. Show pictures of your company that demonstrate you are fun, likable, hardworking, patriotic, and friendly.

By continually examining and learning from the data generated by your Instagram work, you have the opportunity to get closer to your customers and gain new insights. One warning—don't get paralyzed by it all. Use the data as a supplement to common sense and your basic business insights. Let it sharpen your skills and help you be a continual learner, not continually second-guessing yourself.

THE SNAPSHOT

(1) Look into your analytics and determine the number of visitors coming to your website from a mobile device. (2) Plan on that number doubling in the next year or two. (3) Begin taking the steps necessary to make your mobile user experience as enjoyable as the desktop experience. (4) Create a short list of goals that you want to monitor and then strive to reach them. Let analytics help drive your decisions.

Conclusion
Charlie Chaplin Versus John Gilbert

I've tried to make the case throughout this book that the online world is going mobile. I've described that massive transition as clearly as I could. I've attempted to outline how Instagram can help you make a successful transition. It can be the tool that helps you step foot into the new world. You can fight against the mobile future if you want, but it is inevitable. The only question is, *Can you put down this book and begin taking steps to successfully cross over into the new format?* It is not an exaggeration to say that the success of your company probably depends on it.

There was a massive transition in another industry almost a hundred years ago. It might provide a helpful lesson. In 1927, movies went from silent to talkies. That transition had a direct impact on the actors involved, just like the transition to mobile is going to have a direct impact on every website owner currently online. But the transition and how it impacted Hollywood stars might surprise you.

Film critics seem to agree that it is a longstanding Hollywood myth that the transition to talkies killed the careers of the silent-era actors. Countless critics, such as Gary Susman of the *Moviefone* blog, have pointed out that many actors made the transition very nicely.

But it is also true that many larger-than-life stars did not make the transition. Many stars had acquired enormous success in the silent movie era but were ultimately rejected by audiences in the new talkie era because their voices were not well suited for the medium. Many had heavy Eastern European accents, Brooklyn accents, or voices that simply didn't seem believable.

One very prominent silent movie star, John Gilbert, was famous for having his first talkie film present his voice in such a high pitch that audiences were shocked. Later, the audio technicians took full responsibility and said that his voice was presented incorrectly due to their technical difficulties with the new audio recording technology. He went on to do a few more talkies, but his career never recovered. His talents in the silent era generated a very large following, but those fans drifted away because of his inability to cross over into the new format.

Then there was Charlie Chaplin. Chaplin was a huge star of the silent era. He cofounded United Artists, a business move that gave him complete control of his films. He would write, direct, produce, edit, score, and star in his movies. By 1918, he was one of the wealthiest men in the world. But even well into the talkie era, Chaplin refused to make the transition. He didn't support the new format and was uninterested in working with it. He continued to release silent movies throughout the 1930s, and he didn't release his first talkie until 1940, more than a dozen years after the talkie era started. His first talkie, *The Great Dictator*, was a hit—in fact, it was his most commercially successful film. Even though he was late to make the transition, when he did, he did it with perfection. He spent massively and ensured that his first talkie was a great movie. Sadly though, over the decade of the 1940s, Chaplin fell out of popular appeal with U.S. audiences. His reign as a top star was over. The transition proved difficult even for him.

So did talkies kill the careers of silent movie stars? No, not really. What really happened was pretty simple. The stars that were fresh, young, and energetic made the leap from silent movies to talkies and went into the new era with enthusiasm. Many of them became the superstars of the next era. Sadly, the stars that were generally older and had more well-known brands were also tired and battling personal demons. They didn't make the transition well. It was a gulf they couldn't cross. Chaplin, because of his great wealth and incredible perfectionism, was able to bridge the gap, but even his influence significantly declined in the coming decade.

So our cautionary tale has four types:

1. Fresh young actors ready to jump into the new format. They were not marquee names yet, but they would become the stars of the new talkie format.

2. Older established stars, like John Gilbert, who had extensive followings and marquee names. But "technical difficulties" sabotaged their ability to enter the space.

3. Established stars who were very prominent in the silent era, were tired, tied to the old ways, hampered by personal demons, and unable to re-create themselves in new era.

4. Charlie Chaplin, so rich he had the ability to wait 13 years, but ultimately entered the space. His decision to wait wasn't the right approach, but he was able to buy his way out of his mistake and perform fairly well in the new format.

Which actor are you in the drama of jumping from a desktop presentation of your brand to a mobile presentation? Of course, movie stars have shorter careers than most companies' brands have influence. But the similarities between the two industries are significant enough to give us all reason to think hard. Questions to consider include:

- Is your brand fresh—meaning, is it ready to make the leap to mobile platforms?

- Are your images tired?

- Are your systems for taking pictures and getting them approved for use painfully slow and uncreative?

- Does internal bureaucracy stifle your use of photography?

- Are your branding strategies energetic and creative?

- Are technical difficulties going to destroy your ability to cross over into the new format?

Using Instagram as a tool to jump into the new mobile format can be a simple step toward your eventual success in this exciting new space. Let me leave you with a final snapshot of how to get up and running quickly.

1. Set up an Instagram account for your business.

2. Choose a profile picture and description that clarifies who you are and what you're all about.

3. Determine your ideal Instagram followers and determine the types of images they would appreciate seeing.

4. Upload an initial collection of those ideal images so that your account has some content. Make sure it is very nice-quality imagery.

5. Explore the apps available to help you improve your photo editing skills.

6. Invite your existing fans, followers, and newsletter subscribers to begin following you on Instagram.

7. Consider holding a contest as an incentive for your existing fans and followers to jump into Instagram and begin following you there.

8. Now that you have "your tribe" following you, set a goal of growing your Instagram profile to a respectable size. If you have a few hundred followers at this point, then consider shooting for the goal of 1,000 followers.

9. Identify your niche or industry participants within Instagram and start following the most prominent people or their followers. Set the goal of following 10 to 20 industry insiders per day.

10. Identify the images common within your industry and the hashtags associated with the images.

11. Use common industry hashtags to extend the reach of your images. Set the goal of publishing one or two relevant images a day, with the appropriate hashtags.

12. Use common industry hashtags to explore new pictures and new users. Set the goal of liking 100 relevant images per day.

13. Comment on images that use hashtags relevant to your industry. Set the goal of leaving three to five comments a day.

14. Use the tools outlined in Chapter 17 to integrate your Instagram work into your website and other social media sites, especially

Facebook. Make it easy for your fans and followers on those sites to migrate to Instagram.

15. Explore simple ways to use Instagram to generate revenue.

16. Learn to make display ad–style images in Photoshop Elements and occasionally announce a product, contest, sale, or special deal on Instagram. Learn to drive traffic from Instagram onto your e-commerce sites.

17. As part of your next product launch, consider how the visual product launch strategy can be used to engage prospects on Instagram.

18. Identify ways you can use the geotag information or hashtag information on Instagram to expand your customer interaction and involvement. Explore ways to make your next event "Instagram friendly."

19. Treat Instagram as your first endeavor into the world of mobile marketing. Consider how your website performs, your traffic behaves, and your customers interact. Plan for a vibrant mobile marketing future.

Is connecting to your ideal prospect easier than you think? It might be. Frigyes Karinthy originally suggested the idea that everyone in the world is within six degrees of separation or less. In other words, it would take less than six personal introductions for you to meet any specific person on the planet. In 1967, American psychologist Stanley Milgram conducted a set of experiments that showed that people in the United States are connected by approximately three friendship links. Is it possible that every prospective customer in your niche or industry is just three introductions away from learning about you? If that's true and if Instagram can help make the connection, then your future will certainly be bright.

I sincerely wish you all the best on your Instagram and mobile marketing efforts. If you'd like to stay connected, get additional resources, and learn about our latest discoveries, then visit us at http://www.instagrampower.com. We'd love to hear from you and help you continue on your journey.

Index

About the Author

Jason G. Miles is the creator of the Power Book series, a collection of books dedicated to providing exceptional content for work-at-home marketers. His second book in the series—*Craft Business Power*—is an Amazon number one bestselling book in the e-commerce and web-marketing categories. His first book in the series—*Pinterest Power*—is also an Amazon bestseller.

Jason is the vice president of advancement (marketing, fundraising, and human resources) at Northwest University in Seattle, Washington. He holds a master's degree in business administration and undergraduate degrees in both organizational management and biblical studies. He also teaches as an adjunct professor in the School of Business Management.

In 2008 Jason cofounded Liberty Jane Clothing with his wife, Cinnamon, and serves as the company's primary marketer. To date, over 250,000 digital guidebooks have been downloaded from Liberty Jane Clothing's e-commerce website. The company is a thriving six-figure online business. With a cultlike social media following, Liberty Jane has grown to include a Facebook fan page with over 27,000 likers, a Youtube channel with over 9,600 subscribers and 1.7 million video views, a Pinterest profile with over 7,000 followers, and an Instagram profile with over 1,750 followers.

In 2011 Jason started http://www.marketingonpinterest.com, a blog dedicated to helping small business owners and marketers grow their businesses on Pinterest. His Pinterest Boot Camps and his free e-book, *The Ultimate Pinterest Marketing Guide*, have led the industry.

Jason also leads an active consulting practice and loves helping entrepreneurs go from concept to cash. In 2012 he worked with over 1,000 small business owners to launch or grow their new businesses. As a frequent conference speaker and workshop leader, Jason leads marketers in exploring practical ways to leverage social media. More information is available at http://www.instagrampower.com. You can follow Jason on Instagram @mrjasonmiles and on his blog at http://www.marketingonpinterest.com.